ord

fr

CONCILIUM

THEOLOGY IN THE AGE OF RENEWAL

CONCILIUM

CONCILIUM / VOL. 18

CANON LAW

RELIGIOUS FREEDOM

Volume 18

1-0313

CONCILIUM
theology in the age of renewal

PAULIST PRESS
NEW YORK, N.Y. / GLEN ROCK, N.J.

The Imprimatur for this volume applies
only to articles by Roman Catholic authors.

NIHIL OBSTAT: Joseph F. Donahue, S.J., S.T.L.
Censor Deputatus

IMPRIMATUR: ✠ Bernard J. Flanagan, D.D.
Bishop of Worcester

September 26, 1966

The Nihil Obstat and Imprimatur are official declarations that a book or
pamphlet is free of doctrinal or moral error. No implication is contained
therein that those who have granted the Nihil Obstat and Imprimatur agree
with the contents, opinions or statements expressed.

Library of Congress Catalogue Card Number: 66-29260

Suggested Decimal Classification: 291.8

BOOK DESIGN: Claude Ponsot

Paulist Press assumes responsibility for the accuracy of the English trans-
lations in this Volume.

PAULIST PRESS
EXECUTIVE OFFICES: 304 W. 58th Street, New York, N.Y. and 21 Harris-
town Road, Glen Rock, N.J.
Executive Publisher: John A. Carr, C.S.P.
Executive Manager: Alvin A. Illig, C.S.P.
Asst. Executive Manager: Thomas E. Comber, C.S.P.

EDITORIAL OFFICES: 304 W. 58th Street, New York, N.Y.
Editor: Kevin A. Lynch, C.S.P.
Managing Editor: Urban P. Intondi

Printed and bound in the United States of America by
The Colonial Press Inc., Clinton, Mass.

CONTENTS

vii

PART II

BIBLIOGRAPHICAL SURVEY

PART III

DO-C DOCUMENTATION CONCILIUM

PART I
ARTICLES

Joseph Lecler, S.J. *Paris, France*

Religious Freedom:
An Historical Survey*

Vatican Council II's *Declaration on Religious Freedom* states that this doctrine is rooted in divine revelation. This statement applies to revelation in its last and definitive state, to the message of Christ which the apostles were charged to proclaim to the whole world. In the Old Testament, the People of God was established as a nation and still accepted the law which held sway throughout the ancient world, namely, that religion is so closely intertwined with the political structure that any religious offense, particularly any conversion to an alien worship, was subject by law to the same penalties as civil offenses. The Mosaic law lays down most severe punishments for such things as blasphemy (Lev. 24, 15-16), idolatry (Deut. 13, 6-11; 17, 2-7) and false prophecy (Deut. 13, 2-6).

The religion of Christ, on the contrary, is no longer connected with any nation as such. It is a universal religion, autonomous in its own spiritual sphere, and it proclaims itself as a religion of freedom, as St. Paul said repeatedly. The Christian was free with regard to the obligations of Jewish law (Gal. 4, 1-5. 13) and free with regard to the Roman State: he respected its laws

* In order not to encumber this article with references, may I point out that all the quotations and facts mentioned here can be found with their exact references in my two-volume work, entitled: *Toleration and the Reformation* (tr. T. L. Westow) (London: Longmans; New York: Association Press, 1960).

3

and paid his taxes, but, as Christ had said, if he gave to Caesar what was Caesar's, he also knew that he had to render unto God what was God's (Mt. 22, 21). St. Peter and the apostles used the same language: "We must obey God rather than men" (Acts 4, 19; 5, 29).

Since Christianity is in principle a religion of the inner life, it emphasizes the human conscience. This conscience is both a guiding light in our life and a judge of our actions. St. Paul relates it to charity and faith, saying that its aim is "love that issues from a pure heart and a good conscience and sincere faith" (1 Tim. 1, 5). It is this love which should make a Christian deal gently with "weak" consciences and not shock them with the claim that they suffer from wrong opinions, remnants of their previous beliefs (1 Cor. 8, 1-13). As for faith, conscience can only approach it in freedom. Christ does not force anybody. He preaches, he teaches, he invites, but he leaves the person free: "If you want to . . ." (Mt. 19, 21-22). Even his miracles do not prevent a man from deciding for himself. St. John observes that "though he had worked so many signs in their presence, they did not believe in him" (Jn. 12, 37). When a village does not want to receive him, he passes on without insisting (Lk. 9, 55). The apostles are told to do the same when setting out on their mission (Mt. 10, 14. 15). Is it necessary to point out that the *compelle intrare* (make them come in) in the parable about the discourteous behavior of those invited (Lk. 14, 23) has nothing to do with permission to use compulsion toward unbelievers, schismatics and heretics? It needed the imagination of a St. Augustine to suggest such an interpretation.

Within the life of the Church, freedom is obviously not without limits. It must be tempered with charity (Gal. 5, 13) and discipline. The latter may go as far as excommunication (Mt. 18, 17; Tit. 3, 10; 1 Tim. 1, 20), but this does not go beyond a simple exclusion from the community. When St. Paul threatens the incestuous Corinthian in this manner (1 Cor. 5, 13) and quotes the text of Deuteronomy in support: "Take the evil one from the midst of you," he does so only in order to transform into spiritual punishments the terrible punishments laid down by Moses for idolatry, adultery and rape (Dt. 17, 2-7; 22, 32; 24, 7). The carnal weapons of the old law are done away with to make room for purely spiritual weapons (2 Cor. 10, 4). During the course of the centuries the same lesson has been drawn from the parable of the weeds (Mt. 13, 24-30. 36. 43): no violence must be used against sinners or heretics. When the weeds have been sown among the good seed, we must "let both grow together until the harvest". The weeds will not be thrown into the fire until the end of the world.

The Patristic Era

The new law is truly alive with this spirit of freedom. Its authenticity was reflected in the texts of the ancient Church at the time of the persecutions. Not only was the Church separated from the State but it was subjected to legal persecution because it rejected the Roman gods. Rome, like all ancient cities, was closely bound up with its gods. As Cicero said: "Every State has its own religion; we have ours" (*Pro Flacco,* 28). It tolerated the Jews on the ground that they were a conquered nation. It tolerated various Oriental cults insofar as they represented ancient nations that had become subject to Rome's imperial power. But it refused to tolerate Christianity, a universal and independent religion which rejected the indivisible sovereignty of the State and only respected the law in the civil domain.

The most explicit references to general religious freedom among the Christian apologists are found in Tertullian and Lactantius. "It is a matter of both human and natural law," says Tertullian, "that every man can worship as he wishes. . . . It is not in the nature of religion to impose itself by force." Lactantius says: "Nothing is so much a matter of free choice as religion; it disappears and becomes meaningless if sacrifice is offered against one's will." Moreover, while St. Cyprian is the author of the famous axiom that "there is no salvation outside the Church", he also observes that "in the kingdom of spiritual circumcision the Church deals with those that are guilty, not with the carnal sword but with the spiritual sword"; furthermore, even the spiritual sword must be handled with prudence: the bishop of Carthage quotes the parable of the weeds against the upholders of extreme rigorism.

The Edict of Milan (313) may be considered as ending this primitive period of Christianity in which we have already found such a clear expression of the essential requirements of religious freedom: freedom of the act of faith, distinction between State and Church, the radical exclusion of temporal or corporal punishments as sanctions for religious offenses. The edict itself, which was addressed to the governors of the provinces, promulgated freedom for all forms of worship without restriction: "It suits the tranquillity which the Empire enjoys that all our subjects be completely free to adore the god of their choice and that no cult be deprived of the respect that is due to it."

The Edict of Milan and the conversion of Constantine brought freedom and power to the Church. The privileged situation of the Church in an Empire that had become Christian put the Church to a severe test. In fact, the great patristic period provides the history of religious freedom with various and somewhat divergent data. Sometimes the Fathers speak like apologists when they treat of the freedom of faith. At the time of the Arian crisis during the reign of Constantius II, Athanasius roundly denounced the constraint put on the faithful: "The proper character of religion is not to impose itself but to persuade. The Lord did not do violence to anybody. He maintained that everyone is free and said to all: 'Whoever wants to follow me', and to his disciples: 'Do you want to leave, too?' Are we now going to do the opposite of what the Lord did?" St. Hilary wrote in the same vein: "If we used violence to establish the true faith, the teaching of the bishops would oppose us and would declare that God is the Lord of the universe and does not want any forced homage." St. Augustine expressed this freedom in a famous formula that will never cease being quoted: "No man can believe unless he wants to" (*credere non potest homo nisi volens*).

There is also a pointer to this religious freedom in the protests leveled by the Fathers against the intrusions of the State into the domain of religion, particularly when these intrusions tended to work in favor of heresy. Commenting on the Lord's words: "Render unto Caesar what is Caesar's", Hosius of Cordova wrote to Emperor Constantius II: "We are not allowed to assume imperial authority. But you have no power in the ministry of holy matters." Ambrose of Milan put it still more vigorously when Emperor Valentinian II wanted to hand over the Porcian basilica to the Arian Bishop Auxentius: "Don't imagine that you possess an imperial right over the things that are God's. . . . The palaces belong to the Emperor, the churches to the priest." Apart from the classical text: "This world is governed by two powers, the sacred authority of the bishops and the royal power," it is particularly worth remembering the treatise *De anathematis vinculo* where the radical difference between the Old and the New Testaments is underlined. "Before the coming of Christ . . . there were men that were truly both priest and king, like Melchisedech. . . . In the same way pagan emperors have been called high priests. But since the true priest and king has appeared, the Emperor has no longer taken the title of high priest and the priest has no longer claimed royal dignity."

Such a clear distinction between the function of the prince and that of the bishop could have led to freedom of worship and served as a commentary on the Edict of Milan, but the famous edict had long been forgotten. From the end of the 4th century paganism had become the *religio illicita* (the unlawful religion) which Christianity once was. This switch-over allowed the Christian emperors to recover their traditional religious power in the form of Caesaropapism. Like their pagan predecessors, they particularly deemed religious unity indispensable to the unity of their empire. This preoccupation with unity was the more pressing because of the hard times and the threat of invasions. Hence, they not only arrived at the suppression of paganism but at the repression by force of any confessional dissidence. Under Constantius II there was even a danger that Arianism might thus be imposed. A century later this line provided a chance for the monophysites.

It was mainly on such occasions that bishops and popes again used the language of the apologists. However significant these warnings were, they did not prevent Catholic prelates from supporting the violent suppression of schisms and heresies when circumstances had become more favorable. Thus the laws of the empire gradually incorporated heavy temporal penalties, even capital punishment, against the Manichaeans, the Donatists, the Eunomians and the Eutychians. Although rarely applied in their full severity, they nevertheless acquired a place in Roman law where later on canonists could easily find them again.

The Catholic bishops' fear of the turbulent spread of schisms and heresies was a major reason for recourse to legal persecution. Texts, such as that of the priest, Salvian of Marseilles, where the "good faith" of heretics was allowed to support their claim to indulgence, were rare. St. Augustine himself took this view at the beginning of his pastoral ministry. He refused to deal severely with the Manichaeans whom he had personally known. For a time he also believed that gentle means such as preaching and discussion would be enough to bring the Donatists back into the fold, but in the end he left things to the forceful intervention of the civil authority. From then on he put civil and religious offenses on the same level, subject to the same sanctions. It is then, also, that he gives a literal interpretation to the *compelle intrare* of the Gospel, and so joins his episcopal colleagues in ideas that were commonly accepted by them. On one point, however, he remained adamant: like St. John Chrysostom, St. Martin of Tours and the majority of bishops, he refused to allow capital punishment for heretics and schismatics.

Thus the patristic age contributed some clear data for the future: freedom to accept the faith, and the refusal of extreme penalties for the repression of religious offenses. On the other hand, the distinction between Church and State remained in theory rather than in practice. The powers of the emperors in the religious field were only denied occasionally: there was a tendency to object to them when they worked in favor of heresy, but even St. Leo could not find enough words to praise the "royal and sacerdotal zeal" of the "good" emperors!

The Middle Ages

One cannot deal with religious freedom during the Middle Ages without recalling in a few words the sociological structure of the Christian world since the time of Charlemagne. It is not enough to say that it was still linked with the ancient world where religion was part of the whole institutional framework. The word "Christendom", which appears in this social sense since the 9th century, designates a political system based on unity of faith. What made this a "new" civilization was the fact that the Church enjoyed a marked predominance in the temporal world. It differed from the empire of the Caesars in that it was wholly inspired by the Church after a long and obscure process in which many different peoples were thrown together as a result of the invasions. In a very real sense, the empire and royalty on the one hand and the priesthood on the other were like the organs of a unique body, a kind of City of God. The pope was the head as the supreme guardian of the faith.

This structure of Christendom helps us to understand two typical facts of the medieval world: (1) the tolerance in principle, and often in practice, of Jews and unbelievers; (2) the complete lack of tolerance toward heretics.

Jews and pagans had a kind of separate existence in this Christendom. They just were not part of it. The former could be found more or less anywhere, in the Papal States as in the Christian kingdoms. The unbelievers were not exclusively enemies outside against whom the Crusaders were sent. There were Moslem communities in the Frankish kingdom of Syria as well as in the Christian kingdoms of Spain. Obviously, it cannot be denied that there were frequently conversions of non-Christians by force. The most notorious example is the conversion of the Saxons when they were conquered by Charlemagne. But there were always voices raised in protest against the use of such methods, reminding the sovereign of the axiom that every man must be left free to accept or reject the faith.

One of the most famous documents illustrating this point is the rescript of Nicholas I to King Boris of Bulgaria (866). He said that insofar as the pagans are concerned "we cannot tell you otherwise than that they must be persuaded of the vanity of idols by exhortation and counsel, but not by force". If they do not want to listen, leave them alone, but "no violence must be done to them to bring them to the faith". We must act in accordance with the wishes of God who only wants free worship. This text, like the declarations of St. Augustine, St. Gregory and the fourth Council of Toledo (633) on the conversion of the Jews, passed as current doctrine into the canonical collections of the 11th and 12th centuries. St. Thomas sums them up briefly in his *Summa:* "Among the unbelievers, there are some, such as the Jews and the heathens, who have never received the faith. These unbelievers must not be forced into the faith because to believe is a matter of free will" (IIa IIae, q.10, a.8c).

Should this religious freedom of Jews and pagans go so far as to tolerate their meeting for worship and their rites? St. Thomas is rather in favor of the Jews: "There is a real good in that they continue to observe their rites; they are rites in which formerly the truth of the faith was prefigured, that faith which we hold ourselves" (IIa IIae, q.10, a.9). Insofar as unbelievers are concerned he seems at first to have more than just some reservations. According to him, "their rites contain no element of truth or usefulness". Nevertheless, in practice he formulated the principle for a solution which was extended to the Protestant confessions from the 16th century on. In substance this principle refers to the famous distinction of *thesis* and *hypothesis* (to use a terminology that became fashionable in the middle of the 19th century): in itself it is not good that a worship should continue when it is based on erroneous belief, but it can nevertheless be tolerated "either to obtain a greater good or to avoid a greater evil" which would arise from its prohibition (IIa IIae, q.10, a.11). With these ideas Thomas justified a situation which existed in fact: in Frankish Syria and Christian Spain, Moslem communities observed their rites and customs in full freedom. They were even given a legal statute. One of the kings of Castile, Alphonsus VI (1065-1109), even called himself "emperor of two religions". It was only from the 14th century on that the situation of the Moslem communities in Spain deteriorated dangerously.

If it is possible to speak of some genuine tolerance toward Jews and Moslems, the intolerance of the medieval Church toward heretics can only be called absolute. It went much further than the hardships of early Christianity. The death penalty, which horrified St. Augustine, spread during the 11th and 12th centuries and became regular practice in the 13th with the establishment of the monastic inquisition. This change was brought about through the influence of various factors. First of all, there was the influence of the Old Testament: emphatically assimilating heresy with blasphemy, as the canonists and St. Thomas did, was dangerous, for it suggested a return to the shocking punishments laid down by the Mosaic law for blasphemers and idolaters. One also notices the revival of Roman law during the 12th century and the rediscovery of very severe laws which were, however, hardly applied at the time they were formulated. St. Thomas was no doubt influenced by these factors when he assimilated heresy to counterfeiting and the crime of *lèse-majesté* (IIa IIae, q.11, a.3).

However, the decisive factor which sealed the fate of the heretic lay in the sociological structure of the medieval world. Faced with the power of Islam, Christendom had to rely on the unity of its faith for its strength and cohesion. Any attempt at corrupting the faith brought with it a seriously divisive element in this social setup. Like the apostate in Islam, the heretic became an outlaw in Christendom. No doubt, people were free to accept the faith but they were no longer free to abandon it. As St. Thomas put it so tersely: "To receive the faith is a matter of free will, but to preserve it once it has been accepted is a matter of necessity" (*Accipere fidem est voluntatis, sed tenere eam jam accep-*

tam est necessitatis, IIa IIae, q.10, a.8 ad 3). Moreover, he does not just mean moral necessity, since he adds that heretics "must be compelled, even physically, to fulfil what they have promised and to preserve what they have once received" (IIa IIae, q.10, a.8c.). The "criminal" is therefore forced either to see himself eliminated by death or to return to the faith. In that medieval society the acceptance of faith was understood in such a way that the believer was no longer free to go back on his commitment.

The 16th Century

At the beginning of the 16th century the idea of universal religious freedom was still alien to the spirit of the age. The world had changed: Christendom had broken up into nations in the temporal field, and it was soon to break up in the spiritual field through the rise of the Protestant Churches and of more and more radical sects, but all these events could not bring about a sudden change in the social and mental structures of the people and their leaders. In both the States that remained Catholic and in the Protestant principalities the principle still prevailed of a religion that was closely linked with the political setup. In the France of Francis I and Henry II, first the Lutherans and then the Calvinists were treated as heretics. Many of them were sent to the stake. The humanists protested against such a bloody repression but they saw no way out other than by attempting conciliation and "colloquies" which might lead to a restoration of the lost unity. At the meeting of the States-General of 1560-1561 under Charles IX, the Chancellor Michel de l'Hospital still reminded members of the traditional principle: "One faith, one law, one king." In the same speech he had already stated that "it was not the difference in language which separated the kingdoms but the difference in religion and in law which broke one kingdom into two".

Nothing is more significant on this point than the peace of Augsburg which put a temporary end to the religious conflict in Germany. Since the Empire had no real political unity, this peace resulted in 1555 from preliminary negotiations between Lutheran and Catholic princes. It stipulated that their subjects would always be free to choose between the only two recognized religions (Calvinism had been eliminated), but if a subject chose a religion that differed from that of the prince, he would have to emigrate to a State where his religion was accepted, without prejudice to his honor, his rights and his goods. Within the smaller field of the principality the same principle still held sway: the State could only admit one religion. Forty years later the Lutheran canonist, Joseph Stephani, summed up this principle in the famous formula: religion is determined by the prince of the region (*cuius regio, eius religio*). Outside France this formula fitted the exact situation in Protestant England, the old Low Countries (divided into the Protestant United Provinces and the Spanish Low Countries) and the Swiss cantons (divided into Catholic, Zwinglian and Calvinist cantons). But the new formula was already no longer the same as the old one. The more genuinely medieval one put the unity of faith first: it was the faith that imposed itself on the prince, and not the prince who imposed his faith. The formula, *cuius regio, eius religio,* suited the new situation created by the Reformation much better: the prince became in fact the religious leader and he was free to change his mind if he wanted to. Religious power became but an appendage to the prince's sovereignty over his territory. It became more intimately subject to the arbitrary decision of the monarch or magistrate. This regalism of the modern nation-states only protracted for a long time the intolerance of the Middle Ages and that in an even more intolerant manner.

Only in France and Poland, two Catholic States, did there appear in the 16th century some factors favorable to religious freedom in both political doctrine and actual events. The policy of religious unity at all costs was gradually paralyzed by the development and organization of Calvinism in France and by the proliferation of Churches and sects in Poland.

In France the trial of strength with Protestantism was bound to come to a climax. It ravaged the kingdom for thirty years, but it was this very conflict which caused people to query the value of the traditional principle of "one faith, one law, one king", which Cardinal de Tournon still recalled at the colloquy of Poissy (1561). From the beginning of the reign of Charles IX the party of the "Politiques"—as they were called a little later—concentrated on two points: respect for the conscience and the need for a better distinction of the ends pursued by Church and State.

Ever since the 12th century the problem of conscience had become a bone of theological contention, particularly the question of the "erroneous" conscience. But in the climate of that Christendom, with its corporate preoccupations, the excuse of a "good conscience" seemed hardly conceivable when it was a matter of heresy.

In the 16th century the problem became more urgent and more serious with the vigorous progress and consolidation of the Reformation. How could one deny the attribute of a "good conscience" to people born and brought up in "heresy"? How could one ignore the new emphasis on individual (we could say "personal") factors in life, conduct and religion, an emphasis brought about by the humanist approach? The expression "freedom of conscience" already figured in Luther's work, although with severe restrictions: one could not use one's "good conscience" as an argument against the "Word of God" as laid down in the bible. In France this appeal to conscience had been clearly put forward since 1561. At the meeting of the States-General of 1560-1561, a member of the clergy, Jacques Bienassis, Abbot of Bois-Aubry, told his colleagues: "There is no point in wanting to use force in matters of conscience and religion because conscience is like the hand which the more you press it the more it resists, and it lets itself be led only by good reasons and admonitions." That same year the anonymous author of the *Exhortation aux Princes* implored the king: "Sire, do not force our consciences at the point of the sword." A little later the change can be seen in a declaration made by the Chancellor, Michel de l'Hospital, on September 1, 1561, at the Assembly of the Clergy:

"The conscience is such that it cannot be forced but only be taught . . . and even faith itself, when compelled, is no longer faith." The following year Sebastian Castellion, a Swiss Protestant who had witnessed the French civil war, published one of the most moving little books of that age, *Conseil à la France désolée* (Advice to a Desolated France). Recalling the "golden rule" of the Gospel he addressed himself to both Protestants and Catholics: "One has but to ask those that want to force people's consciences: Would you like to have yours forced?, and suddenly their own conscience, worth more than a thousand proofs, will convince them so strongly that they will be left struck dumb."

"One cannot force the conscience." From this argument against the policy of violence there arose quite naturally the decisive demand for freedom of worship, at least in private, for the Protestant religion. This is indeed what the first champions of tolerance demanded. The Abbot of Bois-Aubry asked it provisionally, at least until that hypothetical council would be summoned that would restore unity. Until then, he declared, "we simply have to live in peace while both religions are practiced". The author of *Exhortation aux Princes,* so preoccupied with peace and national unity, saw only one way of avoiding the imminent threat of civil war: "Let there be two Churches in the kingdom." Michel de l'Hospital had spoken at the States-General of Orleans as a humanist. All his hopes of religious unity had been dashed to the ground in October, 1561, when the colloquy of Poissy had failed. A few months later he made Charles IX sign the first edict of tolerance (January 1562). At the preliminary Assembly he was no longer the humanist, but the "politique". According to him, one should not confuse the political unity of the kingdom with religious unity: "The king does not want you to discuss which opinion is better because now it is not a question of deciding about religion (*de constituenda religione*) but about the common weal (*sed de constituenda re publica*); excommunication does not make one cease to be a citizen." He added that if it had been proved that a family can live in peace when the members follow different religions, why should it not be the same for the national community? The State, therefore, like the family, is a natural grouping, clearly distinct from the ecclesiastical community. In the Chancellor's view, religious freedom was based on both respect for the conscience and the partial secularization of the State.

The edict of January, 1562, did not prevent the wars of religion, any more than did the other edicts of pacification which followed each other during the reigns of Charles IX and Henry III. Nevertheless, it would be wrong to underrate the importance of these efforts or the political writing which continued to support them. The Edict of Nantes (1598), which brought the Protestants a limited but genuine freedom of worship, may appear but a final compromise, dictated simply by circumstance; it nevertheless followed the same line as the preceding edicts and even took over the same terms. It thus sanctioned a political ideology which was much more favorable to tolerance than the principles of the Peace of Augsburg. The latter, after all, only gave religious freedom to the princes—or their despotic régime. The Edict of Nantes ensured the peaceful coexistence of two confessions within one kingdom, an almost unique solution at that time, and without parallel in the Protestant world. By detaching the affairs of the State from denominational conflict, it limited by the same token the hold the State could exercise over the conscience and religion of the subjects.

There is no room to deal with the case of Poland at length, but we must pick out the essential features. Protestantism had penetrated into this country without religious persecution during the reign of Sigismund II Augustus (1548-1572). The result was a multiplicity of Churches and sects. Apart from Lutherans and Calvinists, the country served as a refuge for the most radical sects, Anabaptists and Anti-Trinitarians, who were ruthlessly persecuted everywhere else. Poland became, in the words of Cardinal Hosius, the "refuge of heretics". In 1564 he was consulted by the king on a somewhat brazen request by the Calvinists for a decree banning all dissident sects. The cardinal replied: "It seems to me that, since we cannot suppress all heretical sects, it would be better to tolerate them all; by attacking and devouring each other they will ruin each other." His advice was followed: Hosius could not believe he was such a good prophet. If Protestantism disappeared from Poland, it was the result of the multiplication of the sects and of their insurmountable rivalry.

Hosius' tolerance of the Protestant confessions was only a factual tolerance. It became a legal tolerance in January, 1573, at the Diet which preceded the election of Henry of Valois. This was the famous Confederation of Warsaw, where the Polish aristocracy declared: "We who are of different religions (*dissidentes de religione*) commit ourselves in common, both for ourselves and our successors in perpetuity, to keep the peace among ourselves in the matter of religious differences, and we will not shed blood." After the "flight" of Henry de Valois (who became Henry III in France), the true guardian of this pact was King Stephen Bathory (1576-1586), a zealous Catholic. He loyally maintained the political and religious freedom which he had sworn to observe. He is often quoted as having said: "I am king of the people, not of their consciences. . . . God has reserved three things for himself: to create something out of nothing, to know the future and to rule over the human conscience." He intervened effectively when fanatic dissidents created outbursts of intolerance. His Edict of Pskov (1581), which followed the disturbances at Vilna, clearly shows his determination: "It is true that we wholeheartedly desire that all the citizens and inhabitants of our realm profess the one and ancient Catholic faith. But since God has foretold that there would be scandals and heresies at the end of the world, we do not want anyone to be compelled to accept the faith. At our coronation we have taken an oath by which we swore to all the orders of the realm of Poland to keep the peace among those that differ from our religion. It is with a feeling of fear that we have always kept this obligation before our eyes."

Two factors marked the long reign of his successor, Sigismund III (1587-1632), namely, the growth of the Counter-Reformation and the rise of Socinian Unitarianism. While Catholic pressure became stronger after 1624, the divisions among the Protestants within the realm accelerated the rapid Protestant decline.

No doubt, one should not imagine the denominational peace in Poland at the end of the 16th century in too idyllic a fashion. In that country, where serfdom was even more severe than elsewhere, the rural population that had remained Catholic was frequently oppressed by the arbitrary attitude of the lords. However, the fact remains that, even before the Edict of Nantes in France, Poland tried out, effectively and legally, the practical application of freedom of worship.

The 17th Century: The Reformation

I shall have to limit myself by concluding this study of the modern problem of religious freedom with the century of the Reformation. The results will prove modest because it was still so difficult for people of that age to imagine a State that was not tightly linked up with a uniform religion. Neither the Church nor the States were prepared for the great tragedy of the breakdown of ecclesiastical unity in Western Christendom. Even the division into nations in the temporal field was less serious. After all, unity of belief still remained the framework of every nation and every sovereign State. It was this breakdown that caused, almost everywhere in Europe, the bloody persecutions and wars of religion. Lastly, it was only in the large unified States like France and Poland that men came to envisage freedom of conscience, freedom of worship and the disengagement of the State from confessional conflicts, at least as a temporary solution. At the beginning of the Dutch revolt against Spain, it appears that William of Orange took the line of the first French "politiques" in his attempt to found a genuine national State combined with religious pluralism. Unfortunately, he was soon overwhelmed by the intransigence of the Calvinists and aligned himself on the side of intolerance. In The Netherlands, as in England, Germany and Switzerland, the principle of *cuius regio, eius religio* prevailed; this destroyed personal religious freedom and maintained religious uniformity as a constitutive element of the State.

Nevertheless, there were two small countries in Europe where one could observe an extension of civil tolerance in the first years of the 17th century. There was, first of all, the *Majestat,* or "letter of majesty", which Emperor Rudolph II promulgated in 1609 for the "lands that belonged to the crown of Bohemia". It had been requested by the Protestant nobles who obtained a genuine religious statute for the followers of the Reformation. But this new arrangement could not stand the test. Within ten years the Thirty Years' War broke out because of a difference of interpretation of an article of the charter. Brandenburg also had a religious statute given to it by the Elector, John Sigismund. While he was still a Lutheran he granted this statute to the Catholics when the King of Poland gave him the duchy of Prussia as a fee in 1611. When he became a Calvinist in 1614, he was compelled to grant liberty of worship to the recalcitrant Lutherans.

Subsequent history only shows how difficult it was for religious freedom to make any headway in the modern States. It would appear that the Edict of Nantes might have led to a general easing-off, but nothing of the kind happened. In practice, with the exception of Brandenburg, the Protestant world did not move. Later on there would be a great deal of talk about tolerance, but that was mainly to create some understanding between Churches and sects that had sprung from the Reformation. The Toleration Act of 1689 in England was typical of this. It excluded the radical Anti-Trinitarians and Catholics from civil tolerance. On the Catholic side, Louis XIV took the disastrous decision of revoking the Edict of Nantes in 1685. This led to a veritable and massive hatred of the Church of Rome. The attacks of Bayle and the Protestant exiles and of Voltaire and the Encyclopedists still echoed in the 19th century and seemed to identify the spirit of tolerance with skepticism and unbelief.

In fact, the way opened up in the 16th century was the right one: as the recent conciliar Declaration has reminded us, there can be no real and stable religious freedom which is not based on the respect of the human person, on his conscience, on the autonomy of both Church and State and on the determination of governments never to use temporal force in religion's defense or for its elimination. The highest praise which the Protestant Grotius could give to the policy of Louis XIII in the dedication of his *De jure belli et pacis* (1625) lay in the few words addressed to "Louis the Just": *Nec vim affers animis circa divina diversum a te sentientibus* (Do no violence to those that feel differently from you in things divine).

Rabbi Arthur Gilbert/*New York, N.Y.*

Religious Freedom in Jewish Tradition and Experience

I

The fundamental source of religious freedom is to be found in God's intention that man of his own free will seek him and serve him. There is paradox in this affirmation. Both God's omniscience and man's freedom are asserted. In their profoundest understanding of God's nature, the rabbis insisted that faith itself was a gift. However, their respect for the nature of man also required an acknowledgment that man exercised a freedom to respond to God by works of righteousness or to reject God by disobedience. The paradox was articulated in these words:

"Everything is foreseen, yet freedom of choice is given; the world is judged by grace, yet all is according to the work" (Aboth 3, 19).

The rabbis asserted: "Men were not brought into the world to be wicked but to be righteous. God made men upright but *they* sought out many sinful devices" (Sifre Deuteronomy on Ha'-Azinu).

The risk of freedom, of course, is its abuse, but the exercise of freedom in faith results in a growth of man's humanity and in a deepening of his sense of oneness with God. It would seem, after all, that this is what God intends. "All who of their own accord draw near to God, God draws near to them" (Sifre Numbers on the Beha'aloteka). "If a man hearkens to one command, God

21

gives him the power to hearken to many" (Tanhuma on Beshal-lah).

Some rabbis were even ready to suggest that God's power in the world is dependent on man's proper exercise of his freedom. If man does not himself witness to God, then the quality of godli-ness reflected in the corporate existence is, as it were, diminished. " 'You are my witnesses, says the Lord, and I am God' (Is. 43, 12). That is, when you are my witnesses, I am God, and when you are not my witnesses, I am, as it were, not God" (Midrash Psalms on 123, 1).

"When the Israelites do God's will, they add to the power of God on high. When they do not do God's will, they weaken, as it were, the great power of God on high" (Lamentations Rabbah 1, 33).

The rabbis called the perversity that tempts man to rebellion against God the *Yetzer Ra,* or evil inclination. Only at the end-time, when the final redemption will have come upon the earth, will men be relieved of the need to struggle against this instinc-tual proclivity. The rabbis, nevertheless, never despaired of man's ability in this unredeemed world to discipline life or to achieve glory for God's name. Man was not unaided. God provided man with Torah, his law of righteousness, and with an assurance of his forgiveness and saving assistance.

"The Israelites say to God, Lord of the world, Thou knowest the strength of the evil inclination. God answers, Remove it a little in this world and I will rid you of it altogether in the world to come" (Numbers Rabbah on Beha'aloteka).

"It is written: God has made the righteous and the wicked. Why? So that the one might atone for the other" (Pesikta Kahana, 191A).

Although much in life is determined by forces beyond man's control, man is granted by God the one fundamental freedom— the freedom "to fear heaven". It is only in the exercise of that freedom that man can experience God's presence and be pro-vided the added measure of strength that will enable him to cope with his essential perversity. Furthermore, by his righteousness, man makes atonement even for those who are set against him. Ultimately, all other freedoms that men enjoy derive from the fulfillment of this first and primary freedom. For in seeking after God, man must create society, join himself in labor with others, pursue peace and make justice secure. When man, given religious freedom, fulfills the responsibilities of that freedom, the quality of godliness in society is increased. But when man misuses his freedom, acts perversely and coerces conscience, then he diminishes his very humanity and weakens the power of God on high.

II

If freedom derives from God and if the creator himself is willing to risk the possible dire consequences of man's exercise of that freedom, then it follows that the institutionalized Church may also find in freedom a valid method to assure its continuous link with the divine.

Implicit in this formulation is the recognition that the congregation of God, on the one hand, is custodian of God's revelation; on the other hand, however, it is clear that the Word always needs to be understood anew. The Church itself needs to be reformed continually under the guidance of the Word. Man's ability to know God is limited, whereas the nature of life itself is so dynamic that no one formulation of the Word is ever fully adequate to man's need or comprehensive in its embrace of God's truth. Thus, the faithful themselves are called upon to meditate on the Word day and night. Differences of opinion among the faithful concerning the meaning of God's revelation have their value. From such controversy there may emerge a more profound experience of God's reality. Men are one in their obligation to God, but they differ in their comprehension and appreciation of God's Word. There is no scandal in such pluralism. Indeed, the Synagogue Fathers accepted the fact that "every controversy waged in the service of God must in the end lead to a permanent result" (Aboth 5, 20). When two aspects of truth are advocated, neither can be suppressed.

" 'The words of the wise are like *kedorbonot'*, that is, like 'gourds' that are 'given by one shepherd' " (Eccles. 12, 11). Commenting on this sentence, Rabbi Berechiah said that the word *kedorbonot* can be read *kadur bannot*, that is, like "girls' balls" which maidens toss in sport one to another. So it is when the sages are engaged in the study of Torah. One says its meaning is this, another says its meaning is that. One gives one opinion, a second offers another opinion. But they were all given by one shepherd, that is, Moses who received the teaching from him who is one and unique in the world" (Pesikta Rabbati, 8A).

"A great man is not ashamed to ask a small man: 'Give me water to drink.' So the great man must not be ashamed to say to the small man concerning the meaning of God's Word: 'Teach me a chapter, a verse, a saying or even a letter' " (Canticles Rabbah 1).

Just as freedom is granted man by God, so the Church which is custodian for the Word must recognize that freedom in its own ranks is the very procedure that may enable the Word to break forth and find its mark in the heart of man. The Church grows in the richness of its own possession of the Word in the measure that it grants freedom to the faithful.

III

God's Word obliges man to achieve justice in society and to pursue peace. His Word is for all men; it is not the possession of the Church alone. His covenant was made with the entire people, and not merely with the elders or the priests. Thus, Judaism taught that both the sanctuary and government, the priest and prince, were vessels of God's grace. They were both under his judgment and the instruments through which his will for mankind could be achieved:

"God says, Who has ever come into a synagogue and not found my glory there? Not only that, said Rabbi Aibu, but if you are individually in a synagogue, God stands by you" (Deuteronomy Rabbah on Ki Tabo 7, 2).

" 'And behold it was very good' (Gen. 1, 31). Resh Lakish said, 'Behold, it was very good.' This is the rule of God. The addition of the word 'and' suggests the earthly kingdom. But is the earthly kingdom also considered good? [This Midrash was composed when Edom (Rome) ruled over Palestine and the government was considered oppressive.] Strange! Yes, for it exacts justice of mankind. As it is said, 'I made the earth and created man upon it' (Is. 45, 12). [The Hebrew word for 'man' is Adam. Here, by a slight change of vowels, it is pronounced Edom. The intention of the text then is to read, 'I made the earth and created government upon it']" (Genesis Rabbah on Bereshit 9, 13).

The rabbis interpreted Zechariah's vision (4, 1-6) as prototype of an ideal relation between Church and State. A menorah representing the community of Israel receives an unfailing supply of oil from two olive trees—symbolic of God's divine grace communicated through the prince and the priest. The role and authority of Church and State are distinct, yet both serve God's will and together replenish the lamp of the community.

Although God may be found in the sanctuary and although the existence of government is of his will, the manner in which men use these institutions comes under God's judgment. In the prophetic tradition both the priest and the prince were subject to scathing criticism and denunciation. Both Church and State are called to serve God's law.

The rabbis were particularly disturbed, however, when the instrumentalities of sanctuary and government were placed in the hands of one authority. Political power when sanctified is often oppressive, and religious authority, when bent to the secular purpose, shrinks in spiritual content. While both the Church and State share a concern for the moral well-being of society, their methods of achieving the end purpose are different. The Church makes use of prayer and sacrament, moral exhortation and spiritual learning. It offers the experience of God's presence and provides a method for individual and corporate atonement. The State exercises coercive power. It legislates law, maintains courts and a police force, levies taxes and fines, organizes schools and fulfills its obligation for justice through works of social welfare.

Both Church and State also have dimensions of responsibility that are unique in themselves. The Church faces Godward and its influence is inner and spiritual. The State faces corporate humanity and its influence is external and social. Church and State, therefore, are frequently in tension with each other. The Church must stand in judgment of the State in the name of God, even as the State compels churchmen to consider how that Word of God can be made manifest in society's complex corporate dimension. Both Church and State inspire each other to know the Word of God in a more profound way.

Obviously, therefore, Church and State are obliged to be in dialogue with each other and to cooperate in serving the common good. However, it would be disastrous were they to be joined in one instrumentality or were the one to restrict the freedom of the other.

IV

What is the freedom, then, that Church and State must allow each other and in what ways must statesmen and churchmen restrain themselves in the exercise of power?

Jewish tradition can offer only partial answers to such questions since Jewish experience has been so delimited. Biblical Judaism reigned supreme in a period when most of the citizens of the nation paid fealty to the cultic authorities of the State's established religion. Rabbinic Judaism developed in a period when Jewish conscience was violated and the community oppressed by Christian Church-State alliances. Contemporary Judaism was nurtured in Western Europe at a time when secularistic liberal philosophies were the vanguard of the democratic revolution. With the emergence of the secular State and the diminishing of Church power, the Jews gained a freedom and dignity they had lacked in Europe under Church domination. In America, particularly, the establishment of Church-State separation as a response to the demands of religious pluralism stimulated a growth and a vitality of religious commitment unparalleled in recent history. On the other hand, the achievement of the State of Israel has unleashed such an overwhelming pent-up sentiment of Jewish pride that there is little patience in Israel at this moment for any suggestion that the State become secular in its function. Many Jews are convinced that the State ought to remain Jewish in its sympathy, structure and influence, although providing in every way for the religious freedom of others.

Contemporary Jews chafe in the Soviet Union where an absolute separation of Church and State masks a profound hostility toward religion. Yet they flourish in America where Church-State separation benefits from an American-type secularism sympathetic to much of the spirituality rooted in the Judaeo-Christian heritage. Jews enjoy liberty in the establishment of the Anglican Church in England but fear the outrages of anti-Semitism in the Catholic-influenced environment of Argentina. Having adapted themselves in a defensive way to such variegated realities of Church-State arrangement, Jews have reached no consensus as to the institutional pattern that will best preserve freedom. It is clear, nevertheless, that the achievement of freedom may depend less on the actual institutional arrangements and more on the commitment of religious and political leaders to pluralism as an opportunity for growth in truth. Respect for the integrity of man's conscience and the freedom granted him by God is evidently a most decisive factor in determining how democratic or progressive Church and State will be.

If Jews are not in agreement on a philosophy of Church-State relations, they are certainly capable, with the wisdom gained from centuries of abuse, of making judgments regarding those arrangements that have restricted our liberty, coerced our conscience and violated that which is divine in our right to freedom of religious expression. When God's People raise their voice in protest at restrictions on our religious freedom, then men of goodwill everywhere ought to join us in seeking redress of the wrong. Jews hope that churchmen, at least, will repair the abuses on freedom that still prevail in "Christian countries" throughout the world.

Although Judaism has no clearly defined theology applicable in detail to the many Church-State questions that have erupted throughout the world, there are, nevertheless, rudimentary teachings in Judaism that are suggestive; there are also historic experiences that are decisive in forming a Jewish attitude. It is no secret that Vatican Council II's discussions on religious freedom ranked almost as important in Jewish thought as the statement on Judaism itself, for reconciliation with the Jew requires that the Catholic Church repudiate any intention ever again to coerce conscience and to use force against dissenters. It is required that the Catholic Church instead vow its respect for the dignity of the individual and affirm its regard for the rights of other religions in corporate fashion to profess, teach and publicly communicate their convictions concerning God's revelation for mankind. We are satisfied that, in the Council's *Declaration on Religious Freedom,* the Catholic Church has made such a forward leap through the centuries.

V

In the biblical and rabbinic periods, Judaism had to confront, in a rudimentary way, the question of that degree of liberty it would grant pagans and idolators. The Jewish Commonwealth had to make judgments concerning their existence and right to be. It must be acknowledged immediately, of course, that Jewish behavior was not always exemplary. We are aware that during the period of the Hasmonean Dynasty, for example, Jewish rulers assumed for themselves the office of the high priesthood and also forcibly converted conquered nations. The rabbis were outraged. Indeed, such behavior was one of the central issues in the conflict between the sensitive and liberal Pharisaic party and the Hasmonean household. The Jewish historian, Heinrich Graetz, considers the ultimate destruction of the Jewish State to have been the inevitable consequence and punishment for this intolerance against other faiths (Vol. II, pp. 8-9).

Jewish bitterness during the period of the Roman rape of Palestine produced a religious legislation sharply restrictive of Jewish-Gentile social intercourse and derogatory, in the extreme, of the Gentile's humanity.

In the bloody period of the Christian Crusades and Inquisition, many Jews held a dim view of Christianity. Such arrogant judgments concerning others, however, are exceptions to the rule and not the normative attitude in Judaism. They are certainly not the ideal teachings of Judaism with regard to the integrity of conscience and the depth of religion that may be in the possession of the Gentile.

While Jews prayed that the Gentile would abandon idolatry, they nevertheless recognized, in his persistence, a sign of God's long suffering, and if God could abide such transgression, then, certainly, the Jew must also.

"It has been taught: If a man sees an idol, he should say, 'Blessed is he who is long suffering to those who transgress his will.' If he comes to a place where idolatry no longer prevails, he should say, 'Blessed is he who has caused idolatry to have ended in our lands.' So may it please the Lord to turn the hearts of idolaters to . . . serve thee with a perfect heart" (Ruth Rabbah 3, 2).

Jewish law clearly enjoins the Jew to provide the Gentile with every civil liberty and human right to which he is entitled as a human being and, in fact, to behave toward the Gentile with an added measure of graciousness and loving kindness in order to make a witness to the living God.

Poor Gentiles were granted the right by Jewish law to glean and participate in organized Jewish charities. They are to be greeted on their festivals. Gentiles, but not Israelites, could be helped in their field labor during the sabbatical year when Jews were required to permit their lands to lay fallow. It is worse to rob a Gentile than a Jew because one thereby profanes the name of heaven.

The rabbis taught that God accepted the sacrifices of pagans to their idols as an acceptable offering when they performed their rites with sincerity and purity of heart. In fact, the prophetic tradition used the example of the devotion of the idolaters as a rebuke to the Jews who knew by experience the power of God but were haphazard in their devotion (cf. "Commentary on Malachai 1, 11" in *The Twelve Prophets* [Soncino Press], p. 339).

Furthermore, God's holy spirit rested upon every man according to his deeds (Tanhuma de be Eliyahu, p. 48). The righteous among the pagans were as equal in God's eyes as the Jewish high priest (Sifra, 86B; see also Sanhedrin, 89A and Babba Kamma, 38A).

"God said to Moses: Is there respect of persons with me? Whether it be Israelite or Gentile, man or woman, slave or handmaid? Whosoever doeth a good deed shall find the reward at its side" (Yalkut on Leviticus 18, 5).

During the darkest moment of Jewish history, when Christian coercion wreaked havoc on the Jewish community, Jews acknowledged that Christians were to be considered a people in association with God. In fact, were it not for Christian fidelity to those truths similarly held by the Jews, some rabbis suggested that the Jews might have not been able to maintain their faith so diligently throughout the centuries.

In 1450, the rabbinical scholar, Joseph Yaabez, observed: "The Christian nations of the present day believe in the creation of the universe, in the virtues of the patriarchs, in the Torah from heaven [i.e., revealed religion], in Eden, hell and the resurrection of the dead. Blessed be the Eternal, the God of Israel, who left us this refuge after the destruction of the Second Temple; but for this, our feet would slip in faith—God forbid—if the belief in idolatry were still in the world as it once was" (cited by Joseph Block in *Israel and the Nations* [Benjamin Harz: Berlin, 1927], p. 47).

The chief rabbi of Altona, Jonathan Eybeschutz, wrote in

1763: "The Christians among whom we are living . . . believe in the creation of the universe and the divine being, in divine providence and in the law of Moses. . . . It is therefore incumbent on us to promote their welfare, to praise, to honor and to bless them. . . ." (*ibid.*, p. 47).

The most authoritative Jacob Emden, in the 18th century, issued a Response whose sentiment remains valid still: "The Nazarenes . . . have many precious qualities and honest pious customs; hate and revenge, injuring even an enemy, their pious ones avoid. Happy are they and happy are we if they treat us according to their religion. . . . Jesus brought a double boon into the world. He destroyed idolatry and removed the graven images from the nation; he laid upon them the seven Noachian Commandments and also the Ten Commandments, so that they shall not be like the beasts of the field; and, secondly, he has given them moral precepts and he has made life even more difficult for them than the Mosaic law" (*ibid.*, p. 50).

It is clear, at any rate, that the Jews were enjoined to strive for unity in faith and justice among men, not by instruments of coercion but, rather, by the example of the ethical qualities of their own corporate life. Maintaining their ethnic particularity in the family of nations, Jews hoped that the testimony of their faith would lead other men to the service of God.

Jews would not deny that other nations were in association with God. All nations could have a portion in the time to come, and God fulfilled his own purposes by associating with men and nations even to the ends of the earth. Did he not, after all, emancipate Aram from Kir? Did he not send Jonah to preach repentence to the hated Ninevites? Nevertheless, the Jew felt himself called to fulfill God's law in a particular way as a sign to the nations and as a light to the ends of the earth. The responsibility to witness by example is intended to serve as a restraint, ultimately, on the tendency of one people to coerce the conscience of another, for such a call involves one in service to man rather than rule over man. It respects the freedom of the other to choose his own way of coming to God. Witness is educative, not legislative; it speaks to the heart and mind; it is not coercive. It is a blessing, not a curse.

It is well known, of course, that horrendous outrages were perpetrated upon Jews during that dark period known as the "Constantinian Era", a time when both political rulers and religious leaders sought order in society by an authoritarian imposition of uniformity. Jews emerged as the articulate "no-sayers" to such efforts. We staked our political future on that system of rule that would permit freedom of expression. We remained wary of any religious system that claimed for itself alone the wholeness, completeness and perfection of God's truth.

Although undisciplined pluralism leads to anarchy, it is more to be trusted as an expression of God's truth—fragmented, to be sure, in an unredeemed world—than the programmed homogeneity of Church-State alliances which seek to structure God's redemption on earth through one institutionalized interpretation of his revelation. Thus, Jews have generally resisted Church-State establishments that promulgate prayer for all, favor one religion over another or legislate into law moral codes that are clearly sectarian and frequently repressive. Without question, Christianity, by its insensitivity to the religious rights of others through the centuries, has blemished its own claim to be the sole possessor of God's Word.

We have all seen, tragically and unfortunately, how weakened the Christian Church became in its prophetic function when it depended on the State for its financial support!

VI

Jews have welcomed the revolutionary affirmations of Vatican Council II on religious freedom, even if we remain uncertain as to how some of the principles will work themselves out in history.

We would say "amen" to the assertion that each man is "to be immune from coercion on the part of individuals or social groups . . . to act in a manner contrary to his own beliefs whether alone or in association with others, within due limits". But we would then ask what exactly the Church means by the words "due limits" and who defines these limits.

We would say "amen" to the insight that immunity from external coercion includes "psychological freedom" and that individuals have the right in furtherance of their religious quest "to act in community". But we would then ask what the Church means when it contends that such freedom is limited to "the just demands of public order".

The Church's Declaration is strongest, of course, when it defines the limits of governmental imposition in commanding or inhibiting acts that are religious. It is constructive in its recognition of the State's duty to take account of the religious life of the citizenry. Jews would join the Church in decrying those acts of hostility against religion that characterize Soviet communism; nevertheless, we would ask how, and in what ways the Catholic Church proposes that government show its "*favor* toward religion". Does it recognize a point at which Church dependence on the favor of the government vitiates its vitality? Does it recognize that freedom of religion also requires a freedom *from* governmental-sanctioned and endorsed religion?

Such questions are meaningful because the Church unfortunately has a long history of repression. It has given its support to governmental actions which are restrictive of the rights of other religions. In the name of public order, Church-influenced governments in some countries impose upon the total community, without exception, patterns of Christian sabbath observance, laws of marriage and divorce, acts of censorship and other moral decrees that reflect sectarian judgments and are clearly violative of the conscience of those who do not accept the Church's revelation on these matters.

Jews are still disadvantaged in many "Christian countries" where the faithful control the structures of education and impose rites of Christian affirmation on school children as part of school policy. We are concerned regarding the vitality of the Church and the delimitation on freedom that will inevitably result when the evangelical purposes of one Church or of all Churches are supported through disbursements from the public treasury.

Such violations of conscience seem to find their ultimate support in the Church's conviction that God has fully and finally "made known to mankind the way in which men are to serve him and thus be saved in Christ and come to blessedness". The Church added in its conciliar Declaration: "We believe that this one true religion subsists in the Catholic and apostolic Church to which the Lord Jesus committed the duty of spreading it abroad among all men. . . ." Vatican Council II's Declaration reaffirmed the Catholic Church's conviction that men in society hold "a moral duty . . . toward the true religion and toward the one Church of Christ".

Granted that the Declaration also insists that the truth cannot impose itself except by virtue of its own truth and that religious freedom requires immunity from coercion in civil society, history nevertheless abounds even to this day with examples of violation of conscience on grounds of "public order" and "due limits". This is possible only because there are some who consider their institutionalized understandings of God's truth to be beyond question or change.

Christians are not alone in their capacity to such a lack of charity and openness. In every land, among every people and every religion, there is evident a tendency to establish in the culture the moral views and attitudes of the predominant religion; then, by force of unbending custom, legislation and even police power, the majority imposes these values upon the minority.

Jews are no freer of this human inclination than anyone else. The millet pattern of State-Church cooperation in Israel, for example, works a hardship on many individual dissenters—Jewish, Christian and Moslem. Although favoring and strengthening the authority and power of the recognized religious communities, Israel's law makes it difficult for the non-conformist. Mixed marriages are impossible anywhere in the country. Civic legislation reflecting the influence of Orthodox Jewish political power restricts travel and communication on the Jewish sabbath and the breeding of pigs. It includes censorship of movies and restrictions on autopsies, etc. Defending this policy, Dr. Zerah Warhaftig, Israel's Minister of Religion, explained: "The Jewish State . . . ought not be considered a goal in itself, but rather must serve as a guardian vessel for the enduring traditional values of the Jewish people—the core of which is a religious tradition" (quoted in *Conservative Judaism* [New York: Winter, 1965]).

Even former Prime Minister David Ben Gurion, not known for his championing of Orthodox Judaism, has admitted that Judaism's insistence on "a collection of obligations and prohibitions that embrace a man's whole life from the moment of his birth to his death and burial" has made the controversy about religion in Israel "involved". He adds: "There is a national religion which has absorbed all the historical characteristics of the people throughout the ages, and it is not easy to distinguish between national and religious strains. . . ." Ben Gurion insists that the American solution of separating Church and State, "even though not in an anti-religious spirit, would be no answer to our problem" (quoted in *Jewish World* [New York: April-May, 1964]).

Unfortunately, what Ben Gurion says of Israel is of course also true of Protestant and Catholic dominated countries, as it is of countries under Moslem, Hindu, Buddhist and pagan rule. All men, therefore, are challenged with the responsibility of finding the way to give expression to their own religious commitments and yet, at the same time, remain respectful of the rights of others to pursue God in their own way or to reject God.

VII

The Catholic Church's *Declaration on Religious Freedom* offers the most creative solution I know to the tension resulting from: (1) the absolute right to freedom of conscience, on the one hand, (2) the duty of the State, on the other hand, to legislate on matters of moral concern that affect the just public order, and (3) lastly, the zeal of each religion to win all men to its own particular revelation. The Declaration recommends: "Truth is to be sought after in a manner proper to the dignity of the human person and his social nature. The inquiry is to be free, carried on with the aid of teaching and instruction, communication and dialogue in the course of which men explain to one another the truth they have discovered or think they have discovered in order thus to assist one another in the quest for truth. Moreover, as the truth is discovered, it is by personal assent that men are to adhere to it."

The revered Bratzlaver rabbi once cautioned his followers against contentiousness and coercion as the means to truth: "He whose [primary] wish is to prevail in a dispute cannot possibly see the truth. Indeed, he will give no credence to that which he beholds with his own eyes." Then the rabbi advised: "Fear of the Lord brings truthfulness. . . ." He added: "Falsehoods are many, but truth is one. In the unity of truth there is strength; truth is divine and it will surely triumph" (*Hasidic Anthology* [Block: New York, 1934], p. 488).

There is wisdom here that ought to guide us. Man's duty is to seek God and to serve him as best he knows how. Yet we are also called upon to remain open to that vision of truth cherished by the other.

Where there is justice and mercy, there also will truth be found. Truth is divine; it will surely triumph.

Pietro Pavan / *Grottaferrata, Italy*

The Right to Religious Freedom in the Conciliar Declaration

1. *Formulation of the Document*

The definitive formulation of the *Declaration on Religious Freedom* was achieved through a lengthy process of development. This process began toward the end of the Council's second session, November 19, 1963, with the distribution in the *aula* of the first schema (draft text) on religious freedom, which had appeared as Chapter V of the *Decree on Ecumenism*. At the end of the Council's fourth session, November 19, 1965, the fourth text was voted upon in the *aula*.

It was a process characterized by the considerable number of Council fathers who took part in the development and by the profound and subtle contrasts that arose—contrasts of a doctrinal nature, yet reflective of the various historical situations in which the Church carries out its mission. Also characteristic of this process were the lively and often dramatic pronouncements that animated the conciliar debate and the growing interest of worldwide public opinion.

However, it was undeniably one of the most fruitful processes in terms of positive results. With ever-increasing clarity, it allowed for the gradual delineation of a doctrinal position which was eventually shared and approved by almost all the fathers. The total result of the voting on November 19, 1965 was: 1997 affirmative votes and 224 negative votes. In the public session on December 7, 1965, in which the Declaration was also promul-

37

gated, the result of the voting was: 2308 affirmative and 70 negative. Thus ended the development of one of the most significant conciliar documents—a document which is of historic importance both for the Church and the whole of mankind.

2. Composition and Essential Elements

The Declaration contains fifteen sections. The preface (n. 1) observes that in modern times, because of man's increasing consciousness of his dignity as a person, the problem of religious freedom is posed in *new* terms. Accordingly, the Council believes it opportune to consider and pronounce upon the problem. Sections 2-8 express the fundamental aspects of religious freedom, while in sections 9-14 these same aspects are reconsidered in the light of revelation. Section 15 provides the conclusion: granted the particular characteristics of the actual historical situation, religious freedom constitutes an indispensable principle for an orderly and dignified manner of living together, whether within the individual political communities or between them on a worldwide scale. "Consequently, in order that relationships of peace and harmony be established and maintained within the whole of mankind, it is necessary that religious freedom be everywhere provided with an effective constitutional guarantee and that respect be shown for the high duty and right of man freely to lead his religious life in society" (n. 15).

The essential elements of the document are set forth in summary form in the first part of section 2:

"This Vatican Council declares that the human person has a right to religious freedom. This freedom means that all men are to be immune from coercion on the part of individuals or of social groups and of any human power, in such wise that no one is to be forced to act in a manner contrary to his own beliefs; nor is anyone to be restrained from acting in accordance with his own beliefs, whether privately or publicly, whether alone or in association with others, within due limits.

"The Council further declares that the right to religious freedom has its foundation in the very dignity of the human person, as this dignity is known through the revealed Word of God and by reason itself. This right of the human person to religious freedom is to be recognized in the constitutional law whereby society is governed and thus is to become a civil right."

The elements affirmed in the passage cited are: (1) Every human person has the right to religious freedom. (2) This right has as its object or content an immunity from coercion at the hands of individuals, social groups, or public powers. (3) The immunity is understood in two senses: (a) no one must be forced to act against his conscience in religious matters; (b) no one must be restrained—in those same religious matters—from acting in conformity with his conscience, whether privately or publicly, whether alone or in association with others, within due limits. (4) The right has its foundation in the dignity of the human person as this dignity can be known in the light of revelation as well as through reason. (5) This right demands recognition and sanction in the constitutional law whereby society is governed.

3. Nature of the Right

In the last phase of the conciliar debate the fathers were almost *unanimous* in agreement that *today* the right to freedom in religious matters must be acknowledged for all men. However, disagreement continued to manifest itself in the debates concerning the *grounds* for that right. A consistent and solid minority of the fathers maintained that religious freedom, understood in the sense explained above, should be regarded as a positive *civil right*, ratified out of *motives for the common welfare*. These motives consist especially in three facts characteristic of the actual historical situation: religious pluralism; the basic interdependence among all political communities on a worldwide scale; the ever greater sensitivity of human beings in religious matters. However, these fathers added that should the historical situation change, even the right would cease to exist.

The majority of the fathers instead affirmed that religious freedom should be regarded as a *fundamental right of the person*, *valid always and everywhere, and the Declaration consecrates the majority position in unequivocal terms.* This is also evident from the last sentence cited above: "This right of the human person to religious freedom is to be recognized in the constitutional law whereby society is governed and thus it is to become a civil right." It is clear that citizens already possess the right in question insofar as they are persons; therefore, it must be reaffirmed as a civil right.

4. *Object of the Right*

The object of the right to freedom in religious matters is not formed by the *contents of religious beliefs.* This is also apparent for the obvious reason that whenever a religious belief contains erroneous elements, the impression might be given of recognizing in the believers in question the right to profess and propagate error and hence the right to do evil—since the profession and propagation of error is an evil. This cannot be admitted. "Whatever does not correspond to moral truth," declared Pius XII in his Allocution of Dec. 12, 1953, "objectively has no right either to existence, propagation or actuation." In other words, no one can have the right to profess and propagate error.

However, the most basic reason why religious beliefs cannot constitute the object of the right to freedom in the religious sphere is that rights have *only persons as subjects; relationships between persons and objects or between persons—as in our case —and spiritual values are not juridical relationships;* rather, they are metaphysical or logical or moral relationships. Directly and *formally* juridical relationships are *always inter-subjective,* that is, between subjects and subjects or persons and persons, whether moral or physical.

Moreover, the object of the right to freedom in religious matters has a negative content: a *non-agire,* that is, a prohibition of the use of coercive means. The observation was made many times during the development of the document that the object of any right *cannot be other than good or at least morally indifferent and capable of being oriented toward good.* For the existence of a right in a person *necessarily* implies the duty on the part of all other persons to recognize and respect that right, and, on the part of the passive subject of the juridical relationship, the duty of actuating that object.

Now it is not even conceivable that a person's duty is to actuate an intrinsically immoral object. Yet immunity from coercion is an honorable object, fully in accord with the dignity proper to men insofar as they are persons—intelligent and free beings by nature, with a natural tendency to act responsibly. This demands that in their relations with one another they refrain from using coercive means, especially in those spheres wherein spiritual values are cultivated, and above all in the religious sphere.

Immunity from coercion, as already stated, is understood in a twofold sense: (1) not to be constrained to act against one's conscience; (2) not to be impeded, within due limits, from acting in conformity with it. Immunity in the first sense has always been admitted in Catholic tradition, at least on the doctrinal level, and especially as regards the freedom proper to the act of faith. However, the idea that immunity in the second sense is a person's right has been admitted only in modern times for reasons that will be cited below.

5. *The Subjects of the Right*

The first subjects of the right to freedom in religious matters are men *insofar as they are persons*. Therefore, all men have this right—believers and non-believers. In determining the sphere in which the right can obtain, the fathers made use of the expression *in re religiosa,* that is, in religious matters. This expression was chosen because it was judged suitable to indicate the widest possible scope in such matters. The atheist gives a negative solution to the religious problem. There is no doubt, however, that even this solution falls within the category of religious matters.

In addition, all men have the right to profess their religion both as individuals and in association with others, whether privately or publicly. This stems from the very nature of human beings composed of body and soul and intrinsically social. "The social nature of man itself requires that he should give external expression to his internal acts of religion, that he should share with others in religious matters, that he should profess his religion in community" (n. 3).

The second subjects of the right to freedom in religious matters are religious communities: "The freedom or immunity from coercion in religious matters, which is the endowment of persons as individuals, is also to be recognized as their right when they act in community. Religious communities are a requirement of the social nature both of man and of religion itself" (n. 4). The same section sets forth the extent of the community's right to freedom in religious matters.

First, communities have a right not to be impeded by coercive means from governing themselves according to their own norms with respect to: expression of worship; education of members; establishment of institutions for this end; selection, training, appointment and transferral of their own ministers; communication with religious authorities and communities abroad; erection of buildings for religious purposes; acquisition and use of suitable funds and properties.

Secondly, the right to freedom in religious matters entails that the communities not "be hindered in their public teaching and witness to their faith, whether by the spoken or by the written word", on condition, however, that they do not make use of "dishonorable" means, especially when dealing with poor or uneducated people. "Such a manner of action would have to be considered an abuse of one's own right and a violation of the right of others" (n. 4). This statement is to be interpreted within the framework and in the spirit of the entire document. It is obvious that an abuse of one's right *does not always* result in a violation of the right of another.

Finally, religious communities have the right not to be prohibited from freely showing forth the special value of their teaching by organizing and carrying on activities and institutions in the temporal order (cf. n. 4). It might be well to recall, before proceeding, what is stated in the last paragraph of the same section—even if just for its historical importance. "The social nature of man and the very nature of religion afford the foundation of the right of men freely to hold meetings and to establish educational, cultural, charitable and social organizations under the impulse of their own religious sense" (n. 4).

The right to freedom in religious matters finds its third subject in families, within whose ordinary circle the religious life is the concern of the parents who also have the right to determine the religious education of their children. Hence, they can also choose schools and other means for this purpose. Government must recognize and respect such a right and not render its exercise difficult by means of unjust burdens. "Besides," the document continues, "the rights of parents are violated if their children are forced to attend lessons or instructions which are not in agreement with their religious beliefs, or if a single system of education, from which all religious formation is excluded, is imposed upon all" (n. 5).

6. The Foundation of the Right

The right to freedom in religious matters has its foundation in the dignity of the person considered under a threefold aspect. First of all, this dignity is considered in its historical manifestation. In this regard, the Declaration states that "a sense of the dignity of the human person has been impressing itself more and more deeply on the consciousness of contemporary man" (n. 1). Thus, the demand to act in a responsible manner becomes more acute by the hour, especially in those spheres in which spiritual values are cultivated, and more particularly in the religious sphere.

This demand has even had repercussions—and continues to do so—on the constitutional law governing society. It has contributed on the one hand to the fact that religious freedom in the sense of an immunity from external coercion has been characterized as a civil right, and on the other hand to the fact that public authority is exercised within definite constitutional limits. All this it has done to insure the greatest possible scope to freedom as an exercise of responsibility. Consequently, as just observed, the problem of religious freedom has come to be posed in new terms.

Secondly, the dignity of the person is considered among the constitutive elements of the human being—elements on which it is based or from which it arises. Indeed, the second part of section 2 affirms that men are intelligent and free by nature, *and hence naturally privileged to bear personal responsibility in every sphere* and therefore *also* in the religious sphere. In fact, when it is a question of the relationship between himself and God, man *cannot escape the duty to assume the responsibility* of shaping it personally. "Qui fecit te sine te," exclaims St. Augustine, "non te justificat sine te"—"He who created you without your help does not justify you without your help" (Sermon 169, 11; *P.L.* 38, 923).

This is certainly indicative of a very great dignity—to bear by nature the primary responsibility for one's eternal destiny in such a manner as to be unable to renounce such a responsibility. However, it demands that there be in the religious sphere immunity from every undue external pressure which can have no positive influence in this sphere; indeed, it can only be an element of confusion.

The dignity of man arises also from his relationship to truth. The document considers first of all the relationship between man and truth as a *spiritual value.* Everyone naturally endowed with intelligence cannot fail to notice within himself the demand for, and the duty to grow in, the knowledge of truth—to adhere to it even while he is discovering it and to incorporate it into his life. These are the three moments through which man develops and perfects himself as a person.

However, truth can be known only *in the light of truth* and not through coercive means. Adherence to truth is achieved solely through an act of love; to be valid it must be made *freely.* Incorporation of truth in one's life, humanly speaking, has no perfecting value unless it is carried out as a result of *personal decisions* (cf. n. 2). This is true of confrontations with truth of every kind, and hence also of truth in the religious sphere. As is immediately apparent, the climate in which the three cited moments can be lived in a manner corresponding to their nature and the dignity of the person is necessarily one in which the right and duty of religious freedom is recognized and respected.

Secondly, the Declaration examines the relationship between men and subsistent truth who is the true, transcendent and personal God himself (cf. n. 3). Knowledge of the true God entails at the same time the awareness that he is also the prime source from which all have come and the last end to which all are directed. This end is reached by complying with his law which is eternal, objective and universal—a law which all are bound to know so that they may conform to it.

The knowledge of God and his law is attained through personal study, teaching and dialogue, and the norm that regulates the relationship between men in search of truth is *the norm of sincerity*. This is true both as regards the duty to communicate the truth to others as it makes itself known and understood to one's own mind, and as regards fulfilling the duty to welcome the ideas of others and adhere to them within the limits in which they are true—and *only* within those limits.

However, this demands that there be immunity from coercion when living together, since undue pressures stemming from outside oneself compromise sincerity and encourage falsity and duplicity. At the same time, what the divine law requires in the single and successive moments of one's existence in time is perceived by everyone in the voice of his conscience. Hence, this voice is to be heeded faithfully for the attainment of one's own end, which is the otherworldly and eternal possession of God.

But this also requires that in social relationships there be immunity from coercion, whether in the sense of not being forced to act contrary to one's conscience in religious matters, or in the sense of not being restrained from acting in accord with it. Certainly, as the Declaration states (n. 3), the exercise of religion consists before all else in internal acts; nevertheless, since men are intrinsically social, they are naturally bound, as we have seen, to witness to their religious belief and to profess it in community. Therefore, if they are impeded by force from the free exercise of their religion, a natural need of theirs is frustrated, a right of their person is injured, and the natural order established by God is disturbed.

Thirdly, the relationship between men and revealed truth is also considered (n. 10). A major tenet of Catholic doctrine and one which has been constantly taught is that the *act of faith* by which we are initiated into the supernatural order is one that can only be expressed *freely*. This does not refer to the fact that it can be arbitrarily posited or not, but to the fact that once a person has attained a sufficient degree of knowledge of revealed truth, and while he is aware of the duty to adhere to it, the adherence to that truth can be effected only in virtue of a *free personal decision* strengthened by a special help of God which is customarily called *grace*.

By its very nature, then, the act of faith excludes every form of coercion. "Ad fidem quidem nullus est cogendus invitus"— "Indeed, no one is to be compelled to believe against his will" (St. Augustine: *P.L.* 43, 315). There is little doubt that the social climate in which this can be accomplished, with the least amount of difficulty and in a manner consonant with its nature, is one wherein coercive means in the religious sphere are prohibited.

Hence, in whatever way we consider the relationship between men and truth—whether between men and truth as a spiritual value, or between men and subsistent truth which is the true God himself, or between men and revealed truth which is manifested above all in Christ the divine Word made man—we always arrive at the same conclusion. Men cannot form and live that relationship in a manner corresponding to their nature and to their dignity as persons—that is, *consciously, freely, and responsibly* —unless they enjoy the right to freedom in religious matters.

With good reason, then, it can and must be affirmed that this right is founded on the dignity of the person and is therefore a *natural* right. This remains true despite the fact that it has been fully affirmed only in modern times, when men became more conscious of their own dignity in both the ontological and moral orders.

7. Religious Freedom and Government

The Declaration states: "This right of the human person to religious freedom is to be recognized in the constitutional law by which society is governed and thus it is to become a civil right" (n. 2). In this manner the problem is posed concerning the relationships between the right of persons to freedom in religious matters and civil government. The solution given follows the lines set down in the encyclical *Pacem in terris:* "In our time the common good is chiefly guaranteed when personal rights and duties are maintained. The chief concern of civil authorities must therefore be to ensure that these rights are acknowledged, respected, coordinated with other rights, defended and promoted so that in this way each one may more easily carry out his duties" (n. 60).

First of all, therefore, government is bound to recognize and respect the right to freedom in religious matters. This is implicitly affirmed in the Declaration many times: "Government . . . would clearly transgress the limits set to its power were it to presume to command or inhibit acts that are religious" (n. 3; cf. n. 6).

Secondly, government is bound to safeguard this right effectively, whether by insuring its exercise or by reconciling the exercise of the right on the part of some with the exercise of the same right on the part of others or by restoring it when it has been *injured*. "Government is to assure the safeguard of the religious freedom of all its citizens in an effective manner by just laws and by other appropriate means" (n. 6).

Thirdly, government is bound to promote the right in question and so contribute to the creation of a social climate which facilitates the exercise of the right pertaining to religion as well as the fulfillment of duties with a religious content. "Government is also to help create conditions favorable to the functioning of religious life in order that people may be truly enabled to ex-

ercise their religious rights and to fulfill their religious duties"
(n. 6).

Finally, within the limits set by juridical norms in conformity
with the objective moral law, government is bound to prohibit
the abuse of exercising one's right to freedom in religious matters when this is indispensable for the safeguarding of the *public
order*. This refers to the basic elements of the common welfare,
namely, effective defense and peaceful settlement of the rights
of all citizens and sufficient safeguarding of that genuine public
peace which is had when men live together in true justice and
public morality is duly protected (n. 7).

Obviously, the document delineates an ideal State that cannot
be called *neutral,* much less *secular;* it might rather be desig-
nated as a *lay* State, in the sense that, while not considered competent to pass valid judgments on spiritual values and hence not
even on the intrinsic contents of religious beliefs, it still has the
duty to recognize and respect such values. It also has the task
of seeing to it that citizens do not lack the means to cultivate and
assimilate those beliefs.

This necessarily becomes a service rendered to truth, for if the
right *not to be impeded* from professing their faith is recognized
for adherents of religions which contain even elements of error,
the exercise of this same right will also be assured for adherents
of the true faith. The former will *in this way* obtain *the power*
to propagate even error, *while the latter will have the freedom
to spread truth.*

Further, in the confrontations between truth and error it is
legitimate to presume that, at least in the long run, error will
disappear and truth will be accepted. This acceptance will then
take place in the manner corresponding to the nature of the relationship between person and truth, that is, *in virtue of the light
of truth.* "The truth cannot impose itself except by virtue of its
own truth, as it makes its entrance into the mind at once quietly
and with power" (n. 1).

Lastly, it is recalled that "in the use of all freedoms the moral
principle of personal and social responsibility is to be observed"

(n. 7). Hence, "this Vatican Council urges everyone, especially those who are charged with the task of educating others, to do their utmost to form men who, on the one hand, will respect the moral order and be obedient to lawful authority, and, on the other hand, will be lovers of true freedom—men, in other words, who will come to decisions on their own judgment and in the light of truth, govern their activities with a sense of responsibility and strive after what is true and right, willing always to join with others in cooperative effort" (n. 8).

8. *Religious Freedom in the Light of Revelation*

"The right to religious freedom has its foundation in the very dignity of the human person as this dignity is known through the revealed Word of God and by reason itself" (n. 2). This is an affirmation of the relationship between religious freedom and revelation; the relationship is then examined in the second part of the Declaration in numbers 9-14. Two fundamental points of doctrine are developed: (1) religious freedom as a right of the person to immunity from external coercion in religious matters is not *formally* enunciated in revelation; (2) religious freedom understood in this sense has its roots in revelation.

Indeed, the dignity of the human person, in all its fullness, is known *only* in the light of revelation, for on the historical level it is in virtue of this light that men have come to know with much greater clarity the constitutive elements of their nature. Again, *only* in the light of revelation can they know about their elevation to the supernatural order—an elevation which increases their dignity to an almost infinite degree. Lastly, in this light the composition of the relationship between themselves and God is seen much more clearly.

Actually, it is in Christ—thanks to his teaching and action—that the relationship is revealed in terms of incontrovertible clarity as it really is. It is an *interior, transcendent and immediate* relationship which is fashioned in truth and love, and hence freely in an attitude of personal responsibility that cannot be renounced (cf. n. 11).

Over the centuries the Church has often reaffirmed and always recognized—at least on the theoretical level—the right of men not to be constrained by force to adhere to the Christian religion. This was precisely by virtue of the reason adduced that the act of faith, even though it is obligatory, can only be posited *freely*. For centuries, however, the right not to be forcefully prevented from the external profession of one's religion has not been recognized in Christian civilization when that religion was not the true religion or the one held to be true.

The reason for this is that recognition of such a right presupposed on the part of men a greater consciousness of their dignity, lived and expressed in terms of *personal responsibility*. In other words, there was required the *universal conviction* that rights do not relate *directly and formally* to spiritual values such as truth, moral goodness and justice. Rather, the subjects of rights are persons, and *only* moral or physical persons. Further, juridical relationships are always *intersubjective,* that is, between persons and persons, and not between persons and spiritual values. Finally, the fundamental rights of the person in spiritual values are conceived as immunity from external coercion with the guarantee of the enjoyment of freedom in worship and in the assimilation of such values.

Recognition of this right also presupposed that the greater understanding of the dignity of the person—in the sense of a demand for internal freedom and immunity from external coercion in the exercise of responsibility—should have repercussions on the juridical level and in the exercise of civil authority. In short, it presupposed that men should arrive at the conception and actuation—at least in some degree and form—of "the welfare State". In addition, it was necessary for this *welfare State* to loose itself forever from the currents of thought with which it was bound on the historical level, namely, rationalism, immanentism, monism, positivism, agnosticism, historicism and liberalism; furthermore, sufficient evidence had to be given to show that in its typical elements a State so envisaged could be fully reconciled with the Christian view of life.

It also presupposed—at least such is the contention—that the welfare State should evolve and develop into a *socio-democratic welfare State*—a State which considers itself obligated to pursue the common welfare, contributing to the creation of a social climate wherein not only are the fundamental rights of the person recognized, respected and defended, but also where the indispensable means for the effective exercise of any right and the fulfillment of the respective duties are placed, or tend to be placed, at the disposal of everyone.

The presuppositions in question were verified only in modern times, and then solely through a laborious and very complex historical process often characterized by profound contrasts. Doubtless, a positive influence on such a process was the light shed by the Gospel on the immense value of the human person. "The leaven of the Gospel has long been about its quiet work in the minds of men, and to it is due in great measure the fact that in the course of time men have come more widely to recognize their dignity as persons, and the conviction has grown stronger that the person in society is to be kept free from all manner of coercion in religious matters" (n. 12).

9. *Religious Freedom and the Mission of the Church*

As we have seen, the Declaration affirms that religious freedom has its roots in divine revelation; therefore, "Christians are bound to respect it all the more conscientiously" (n. 9). It also affirms (n. 13) that in political communities wherein religious freedom is recognized and respected as a civil right, the Church enjoys the right as well as the reality of the freedom which is due it by divine mandate and indispensable for the development of its mission. At the same time, the Christian faithful can freely profess their religion and fulfill the grave obligation "ever more fully to understand the truth received from Christ their master, faithfully to proclaim it, and vigorously to defend it, never—be it understood—having recourse to means that are incompatible with the spirit of the Gospel" (n. 14). Such would undoubtedly be *coercive means*.

Hence, "the Church earnestly begs of its children" (n. 14) to place their trust—in the apostolic obligation—first of all in prayer, sacrifice and the Christian witness to life; in the understanding of others, in respect for their personal dignity, in love that is operative, patient and persevering; above all, in the power of the Word of God and in the action of the Holy Spirit in souls. This action is unfolded in accord with a plan of salvation, an expression of infinite love shrouded in the deepest mystery.

Thus, in carrying out this apostolic obligation, "all is to be taken into account—the Christian duty to Christ . . . the rights of the human person and the measure of grace granted by God through Christ to men who are invited freely to accept and profess the faith" (n. 14). It must ever be borne in mind that there is no possibility of embracing truth except in its own light and that there is no growth in truth except in the measure in which one loves the truth.

Lukas Vischer/*Geneva, Switzerland*

Religious Freedom and the World Council of Churches

hen we compare the *Declaration on Religious Freedom* of Vatican Council II with the texts produced by the general assemblies of the World Council of Churches in Amsterdam (1948) and New Delhi (1961), we see at once that there is a large measure of agreement. Furthermore, if we disregard the theological reasoning on which they are based, we see that, insofar as the principle itself and its practical application are concerned, the texts are often almost identical. This similarity is not accidental, and its importance can hardly be overrated, for it points up a convergence of the Churches in facing certain common questions that arise from the constantly changing conditions of modern society.

It is true that the Churches start from different premises. But in their attempt to understand the task of the Church in the modern world they repeatedly achieve common insights on the basis of that common foundation which unites them in spite of all differences. The various declarations on religious freedom are a particularly clear illustration of this. The different premises from which the individual Churches proceed become evident in the diverse arguments advanced in behalf of religious freedom. The World Council shows that no exhaustive argument is possible. Nonetheless, the decisive statement that every individual has the right to confess his religious conviction publicly and that this right must be protected is shared in common by the Churches.

Does this admission create additional responsibility? Shouldn't it be formulated and developed? Is it enough simply to state the fact that agreement exists; shouldn't we rather try to draw the logical consequences? The Churches would not be taking their commitment to ecumenism seriously enough if they did not decide to pursue these issues together.

I

THREE FIELDS OF APPLICATION

If we want to understand in what sense the documents of the World Council uses the term "religious freedom", we have to distinguish three different fields in which it is applied. The discussion of religious freedom currently in progress within the ecumenical movement was originally involved with the question of *Church and State*. The Church must be free from all State control and protection, and even when the Church is not left the necessary freedom to preach the Gospel, it must nevertheless always see to it that the State does not overstep its permissible limits. The discussion then passed directly to religious freedom as a *principle of order within the State,* particularly as a *condition for the life of an international society*. It is from this aspect that the Declarations of Amsterdam and New Delhi develop the question. The more progress the ecumenical movement made and the more deeply the separated Churches became aware of what they had in common, the more urgent the question of religious freedom became in the *relations of the Churches among themselves*. The report on "Christian Witness, Religious Freedom and Proselytism", accepted at New Delhi, examined the issue in this light and showed to what extent respect for the principle of religious freedom is the unconditional presupposition for any communion and intercourse between the separated Churches.

These three fields of application are of course closely connected, and it is impossible to deal with one without indirectly touching upon the other two. Yet they must be distinguished, particularly when we wish to relate the Declaration of Vatican Council II with those of the World Council. *Vatican Council II's Declaration only deals with religious freedom in the second of these three ways,* and while it touches upon the question of Church and State, it does not treat the problem explicitly. The role that religious freedom plays in deepening the ecumenical relationship is not mentioned at all. However much agreement there may be, therefore, we must realize from the start that the scope of the problem is not yet identical for all parties concerned.

II

POINTS TO BE DEVELOPED

Let us briefly survey the earliest beginnings of the discussion within the ecumenical context and select the most important points that have already contributed to the development of our theme.

1. *The Relationship between Church and State*

The inauguration of the ecumenical movement coincided with a much wider upheaval in the traditional relationship between Church and State in the West, particularly within the countries of Europe. While at the beginning of this century one could still cherish the idea that Church and State form a unity and that the Church was in a certain sense the soul of the State and was therefore entitled to certain privileges corresponding to the services it might render, this position became decidedly less tenable after World War I. The political upheavals and revolutions that marked the postwar years; the rapid increase and growing influence of movements, parties and groups that rejected any connection with the Church or were even hostile to it; the more extensive mixing of the population, even in regions where up till then one denomination had predominated; the growing importance of new nations that were anxious to assert their own re-

ligion and culture—all these factors shook the more or less conscious assumption that a given Church could take for granted
that the inhabitants of a given region were its members. This
was certainly not something new. The close ties which formerly
bound Church and State together were already broken in the
18th and, especially, the 19th centuries. But the first decades of
this century did bring about a decided acceleration of the process, and the Churches were no longer able to ignore the fact
that they were a minority within their own nation. This was a
particularly severe realization for the great Protestant Churches
of Europe, for due to historical circumstances they had assumed
especially close ties with the State and had practically no supra-
national bond with one another.

The great ecumenical Oxford Conference (1937) mentioned
this fact mainly as a challenge to the Churches: "The Church
has not yet faced the new situation with sufficient frankness.
With the conservative instincts of all institutions of long standing and influence it has fought a defensive—and on the whole
a losing—battle for the maintenance of as much as possible of
the old ideal of *Corpus Christianum* and of the privileges and
authorities which that implies. . . . The Church finds itself today in a new relation to the community. . . . Domination it
cannot have and possibly ought not to desire. . . . It is challenged to find a new understanding of its duty to the common
life." [1]

2. *The Missions and the New Churches*

This new understanding was not imposed on the Churches
solely from without. It also grew from within the life of the
Churches themselves. The missionary movement, and above all
the gradual emergence of "young Churches", prepared the way
for a new and deeper understanding of the nature of the Church.
Missionary experience demonstrated that the Church must be
understood as a special community called by God for the purpose of proclaiming the message of God's kingdom. The ques-

[1] *The Churches Survey Their Task* (Oxford, 1937), pp. 200-1.

tion concerning the nature of the Church in relation to all worldly and human institutions profoundly stirred theological thought during the years subsequent to World War I. It was becoming increasingly clear that through its close links with nation and State the Church had obscured its own nature and mission; as a consequence its claim to authenticity had to suffer. We only have to recall the sharp attacks launched by the Swiss theologian Karl Barth against identifying the Church with anything that might be labeled "Christian". The authentic meaning of freedom was at the very center of this debate. The Word of God as the sole absolute over against man bestows a freedom such as no human source can provide and as no human society—unfortunately not even the Church, at times—can realize. It becomes real only in the degree to which provision is made for that Word of God.

The debate might not have had such important consequences for the ecumenical movement if it had not assumed practical significance during the rule of Nazism in Germany. The Church suddenly came face to face with a State founded upon an ideology wholly opposed to it. The only way it could proclaim its message was first to liberate itself from the bonds which tied it to the State. The foundation of the "confessing Church" was an attempt to preserve the Church's freedom within a Church and a State that were menaced by a false ideology or had already yielded to it.

What happened in Germany was not without its consequences for the other Churches. They had to decide where and how they could recognize the true Church. The questions evoked by the Church's struggle in Germany were equally valid for Churches in other countries, and consequently it is not at all astonishing that the Oxford Conference of 1937 dealt in detail with the nature of those freedoms the Church could claim from the State. A tentative list of these freedoms was drafted: freedom of religious doctrine, preaching and education, freedom to determine the organization of the Church, freedom to do missionary work and to cooperate with the Churches of other countries and freedom to enjoy the same rights as other groups in the same State, such as the right to property, etc.[2]

The discussion necessarily expanded: the Churches could hardly claim freedom for themselves without likewise claiming it for others. Following the "golden rule", the freedom it claimed for itself would have to be applicable to all. This conclusion was already explicitly accepted by the Oxford Conference: "In pleading for such rights we do not ask for any privilege to be granted to Christians that is denied to others. While the liberty with which Christ has set us free can neither be given nor destroyed by any government, Christians because of that inner freedom are both jealous for its outward expression and solicitous that all men should have freedom in religious life. The rights which Christian discipleship demands are such as are good for all men, and no nation has ever suffered by reason of granting such liberties."[3]

3. International Organization

These considerations acquired additional urgency due to the question regarding the foundations on which an international society could be created and maintained, and insofar as modern technological and ecumenical developments linked individual States more closely together, the need for an answer became more pressing. The founding of the United Nations underlined this need. The non-Roman Catholic Churches found themselves in a difficult position. Since practically all of them were closely associated with some form of nationalism, they could hardly find the principles to solve the problem within the inventory of their own resources. It is therefore not astonishing that the ecumenical movement became preoccupied with the problem. From the very outset religious freedom was considered an essential condition for a viable international organization. The Oxford Conference did not really deal with this in a creative fashion, but all the same it emphatically declared that religious freedom was one of the basic principles: "Freedom of religion is an essential

[2] *Ibid.*, pp. 84-5.
[3] *Ibid.*, pp. 184-5.

element in a better international order. This is an implication of the faith of the Church. Moreover, the ecumenical character of the Church compels it to view the question of religious freedom as an international problem. . . ." [4] The text briefly explained what was meant by this principle and emphasized that Christians cannot exploit the power of their nation to secure unjust privileges within another nation—a statement that was anything but obvious at that time.

But it was not until World War II and the years which followed it that the theme was seriously tackled. During the war (as far as circumstances allowed) the Research Secretariate of the World Council for Practical Christianity made a study on international organization, and the various exchanges in this connection showed increasing agreement on the point that freedom of the individual's conscience guaranteed by the State was a basic principle for the creation of an international community. William Temple, Archbishop of York and later Archbishop of Canterbury, made a remarkable contribution to the discussion.

After the war, the thread was picked up with renewed determination. But in the meantime the context of the discussion had changed. The United Nations had actually been founded, and the *Declaration on the Basic Rights of Man* was receiving public attention. It is against this background that we must see the declarations of the World Council at Amsterdam (1948) and New Delhi (1961). They maintain that every man has the right to religious freedom because of his God-given dignity and that this right must be guaranteed to every individual as well as to every religion and religious group. These declarations specify in detail those rights which involve religious freedom and which the Churches must allow to prevail both for themselves and for others. Of all the statements made by the World Council, these two declarations come closest to that of Vatican Council II. Both the general substance and many individual statements are almost identical. In any case, the conciliar Declaration is partly motivated by this same preoccupation with international order.

[4] *Ibid.*, p. 184.

Among the differences between them, I may point out that the World Council explicitly bases the principle of religious freedom on non-religious convictions.[5]

In comparing the conciliar Declaration with those of the World Council, we should not forget that the latter do not bind the individual Churches in the same way a conciliar decree binds the Roman Catholic Church. Furthermore, although the consensus has been reached and no Church has objected to the statement, not all the Churches have as yet pursued all its consequences. The Department for Religious Freedom and the Commission of the Churches for International Affairs are the two agencies of the World Council charged with studying the problems implied in the affirmation of religious freedom and the practical steps to be taken to translate it into reality.

4. *Contact between the Separated Churches*

One final aspect must be mentioned which has moved the issue of religious freedom into the foreground of the ecumenical movement: the encounter of the separated Churches themselves. For the non-Roman Churches the ecumenical movement was not inaugurated merely to precipitate dialogue. They felt from the start the need to work together as a community. This was particularly acute on the international level, for if the Churches were to bear witness in the international arena, they would have to do so in common. But how could Churches with different and often even contradictory convictions, with different historical backgrounds and different national and cultural characters form a single community? If this was ever to come about, the recognition of the principle of religious liberty would have to be the first and unconditional presupposition. The community could only grow on the common recognition of each other's freedom. The Oxford Conference was clear on this point, although quite evidently it did not pursue the problem and all its ramifications: "We call upon the Churches we represent to guard against the

[5] For a detailed comparison, cf. A. F. Carrillo de Albornoz in *Ecumenical Review* 1 (1966).

sin of themselves conniving at repression of Churches and religious bodies of a faith and order differing from their own." [6] The report goes even further. It regards this mutual respect as an opportunity for Christian witness, since it is by setting an example of mutual tolerance that the Churches actually promote international understanding.

However, it goes without saying that a community of Churches cannot be built on the principle of religious freedom alone. The bonds which link the Churches in the name of Christ are too strong to find adequate expression in the mere recognition of this principle. Yet just such a recognition is certainly a preliminary condition if that deeper communion in Christ is to become visible. Only if the Churches recognize each other's freedom to bear witness can they really meet, grow together and eventually bear witness in common. As their communion deepens and expands, the Churches will observe rules in their intercourse which go beyond the mere principle of religious freedom.

The right to religious freedom is a civil right. When the Churches speak of religious freedom, they speak of rights that are incorporated in civil law and protected by the State for all its citizens. Moreover, although the Churches must respect these rights, they cannot simply confine their efforts to standing by and respecting each other's witness. Their communion in Christ imposes upon them a positive responsibility for each other, and it will lead them farther into a mutual relationship which is beyond that which the law can enforce. This is particularly clear in the problem of proselytism. A Church which tries to attract the members of another Church by non-spiritual means makes it impossible for the Churches to live together; therefore, the practice must be excluded. But actually only the coarsest forms of proselytism are an offense against religious freedom as a civil right; the more subtle forms can only be eliminated when the Churches become aware through the spiritual foundations of their community that they are responsible for each other and contribute to their mutual sanctification.

[6] *The Churches Survey Their Task, op. cit.,* p. 185.

The World Council had to face this problem in all its acuteness. The Churches had founded a community, and each member was aware that he had bound himself to the truth. They were determined to work with each other. What was the result? The Report on "Christian Witness, Religious Freedom and Proselytism within the Framework of the World Council of Churches" (New Delhi, 1961) gave a preliminary accounting. It not only showed what religious freedom would mean for mutual relations between the Churches, but it also stated some demands which were only to be understood as involving an "ecumenical obligation".

Vatican Council II barely treated this aspect of religious freedom. The *Constitution on the Church* and, above all, the *Decree on Ecumenism* and the *Pastoral Constitution on the Church in the Modern World* provide some clues that may lead to a broadening of the issue. An ecumenical discussion is desirable; not only would it clarify the position for both sides, but it could also have numerous practical consequences.

If the discussion is going to be pursued, one question in particular must be treated in depth, a question which has found no answer in the documents of either the World Council or Vatican Council II: How far is the Church itself a community based on freedom? The Church is held together by the common confession of the Gospel. How much difference does this confession allow? Where must we draw the line between a plurality that strengthens the witness to Christ and a plurality that destroys it? Most texts dealing with religious freedom neglect to speak of the freedom that must prevail within the Church. But if the community is to grow and especially if the Churches themselves are expected to set "an example of freedom to all"— as the Oxford Conference put it—then this question is of decisive importance. It cannot be regarded as a purely private matter and be withheld from the ecumenical dialogue; on the contrary, precisely from the point of view of witness it must be included.

Conclusion

Once again we are back to the suggestion we made at the outset, namely that the Churches should formulate their convictions about religious freedom in common and should arrive at an explicit and common declaration of these convictions. While this would certainly provide a broader basis for the mutual relationship between the Churches, it is not the ultimate reason. Such a community could in itself be a witness in a world which is crying out for a more stable order. By renouncing in common every kind of domination, the Churches would be in a position to witness against any power that might claim to be absolute. By their awareness of a common bond and a common service in Christ they would be able to show forth the meaning of this bond in truth. There is no need to stress the value of such a witness in a world whose order is imperiled by a false absolutism on the one hand and is undermined by indifference toward the truth as the source of life on the other.

✠ Neophytos Edelby / *Damascus, Syria*

Islam and Religious Freedom

I t is of course impossible to deal in a few pages with all the problems of religious freedom in the Moslem world.[1] Where Islam remains in practice the only recognized religion, the State applies the teaching of the Koran more or less completely. But most Moslem States today have a democratic constitution which guarantees freedom of religion more or less in the same way as the constitutions of any other modern State. It is easy to understand that this brings about a certain strain with regard to the pure teaching of the Koran.

Before trying to find out how the present Moslem States manage to reconcile the democratic demands of religious freedom with the teachings of Islam, we have to go to the sources and

[1] General bibliography: Shoucri Cardahi, "La conception et la pratique du droit international privé dans l'Islam," in *Recuil des cours de l'Académie de droit international de La Haye* II/60 (1937), pp. 511-650; Willi Heffening, *Das islamische Fremdenrecht* (Hanover, 1925); Henri Laoust, *Le traité de droit public d'Ibn Taimiya* (Beirut, 1948); Theodore Noldeke, *Geschichte des Qorâns* (Göttingen, 1860; reedited several times); Arthur S. Tritton, *The Caliphs and Their Non-Muslim Subjects* (Oxford/London, 1930); Alfred von Kremer, *Kulturgeschichte des Orients,* vol. II, pp. 165ff.; William A. Shedd, *Islam and the Oriental Churches* (1904); D. S. Margoliouth, "The Status of the Tolerated Cults," in *The Early Development of Mohammedanism* (London, 1914), pp. 99-134; François Nau, *Les chrétiens arabes en Mésopotamie et en Syrie au VIe et VIIe siècles* (Paris, 1935).

see how Mohammed himself saw religious freedom and how Islam could coexist with other religions. Accordingly, the thoughts offered here are more doctrinal than juridical in character.

Mohammed's Thought

In general, one may say that in Mohammed's political-religious teaching, even after the institution of Islam, Christianity and Judaism are still considered as basically true, and this gives them a right to freedom and respect within certain limits. Islamic religion with all its beliefs, laws and religious practices cannot be imposed on followers of other religions which, in the theocratic concept of Islam, are seen as distinct and autonomous theocratic nations, though subject to Islam. Faith is the basis of their "nationality", their own religious laws are the only ones that are binding and their religious leaders express, in principle, their exclusive jurisdiction.

The Many Contrary Aspects of This Attitude

As presented in the Koran and the Sîra (various biographies of the prophet), Mohammed's attitude toward other religions is full of contrasts. His conduct is sometimes full of respect, at other times full of threats, sometimes persuasive and then again violent, and this apparently ambiguous attitude gave rise in the course of time to a broad-minded liberalism as well as to bloody persecutions among his followers.

In order to reconcile such clearly divergent policies, traditional Moslem exegesis considers any verse that contradicts the definitive development of Islam's religious policy as *abrogated*. This way of bringing everything indiscriminately into harmony with Islamic teaching may justify itself in the eyes of the believers as filling the need to find a fixed and detailed norm in the Koran, but in the eyes of the impartial historian it distorts the real thought of Mohammed.

Several of these divergent policies could be explained by *op-*

portunist preoccupations. Mohammed, "a preeminent opportunist",[2] was no doubt a man who was supremely aware of concrete possibilities and profitable concessions, even in matters of doctrine. But this opportunism cannot explain everything. Mohammed's attitude toward other religions clearly shows a *slow evolution* in matters of doctrine and politics, conditioned on the one hand by the prophet's increasing knowledge of Judaism and Christianity, and on the other by the reactions of various groups of Christians and Jews in Arabia to Islam at its start.

The Mecca Period

During his first period at Mecca, Mohammed, with his belief in a single monotheism revealed in a holy "book", not only did not realize the essential differences between Christianity and Judaism but was in all good faith convinced that he himself was the inspired apostle of this unique religion among his fellow Arabs.[3] For him there could only be one religion. Only idolaters have no religion at all. During this first phase Mohammed firmly believed that the religion revealed to him in order to preach it to his fellow Arabs was none other than the unique religion which Allah had already revealed to Noah, Abraham, Moses and Jesus.[4] Allah had exhorted them in vain "to establish the one religion and not to split up into sects".[5] In any case, Christians and Jews have only to read the Gospel and the Torah to see that the coming of Mohammed was announced in these books.[6]

However, that opinion was in no way shared by Jews and Christians, and it was not long before the convictions held so dearly by the young prophet were put to a severe test by their opposition. Those "people of the scripture" quoted texts from their "book" which did not conform with his teaching.[7] Mo-

[2] Leo Caetani, *Annali dell'Islam* I (Milan, 1905), p. 205.
[3] Leo Caetani, *op cit.* I, p. 204; H. Lammens, *Mahomet fut-il sincère?*, p. 146; Giuseppe Sacco, *Le credenze religiose di Maometto* (Rome, 1923), pp. 112-3.
[4] *Koran* XLII, 11.
[5] *Koran,* same verse.
[6] *Koran* VII, 156.
[7] *Koran* III, 72.

hammed refused to accept that. Jews and Christians must have falsified "the book" [8] or withheld its true contents from the people.[9] All this forced him in the end to accept the fact that Jews and Christians did not wholly agree with him. His strong sense of monotheism rebelled particularly against the Christian idea that Jesus was the Son of Allah. "Allah could not possibly have a son." [10] "All those who are in heaven and on earth can only be servants of the Most Merciful." [11] What was worse was that Christians venerated angels and "intercessors".[12] They do not differ from polytheism which credits Allah with sons and daughters.[13] Moreover, Christians keep on quarreling among themselves, and they are split up into sects,[14] while there is but one religion, a single one, that of Allah.

The divinization of Jesus, the veneration of angels and saints and the internal quarrels were the main alterations of the book for which Mohammed blamed the Christians. He wanted to bring them back to the purity of "the one religion", but they refused and followed the example of the Jews who had always opposed the reforming prophets sent by Allah.[15]

Confronted with this refusal to reform themselves, Mohammed's whole attitude was one of *resignation*. Allah had said to him: "If they make you a liar, tell them: *My actions are mine, and your actions are yours; you are not responsible for what I do and I am not responsible for what you do.*" [16]

On the day of judgment they will have to answer for their incredulity before the prophet of their nation;[17] he threatens them with the punishment of the last day, and occasionally he treats them as "unbelievers". But during this first period of his

[8] *Koran* II, 70; IV, 48; V, 16. 45.
[9] *Koran* V, 18; III, 64; VI, 91.
[10] *Koran* XIX, 36.
[11] *Koran* XIX, 94; also XLIII, 59. 63-4; IV, 169-70.
[12] *Koran* X, 19.
[13] *Koran* XLIII, 14-18.
[14] *Koran* XLIII, 65.
[15] *Koran* V, 74.
[16] *Koran* X, 42.
[17] *Koran* X, 48.

preaching Mohammed did not once think of maltreating Christians or of driving his followers to fight them: he left their judgment wholly to God.

The Medina Period

Things changed when Mohammed fled to Medina with his followers (the *higrâ,* on July 16, 622). It is this event that turned the simple "preacher" into a national leader and decided once and for all the political-religious constitution of Islam.

The beginning of this period was marked by a broad liberal approach. In the interest of the common cause he considered Moslems, Jews and Christians as one. "Those that have believed [i.e., the Moslems], as well as Jews, Christians and Sabaeans, *all those that believe in Allah and in the last day and do good, will have their reward from their Lord; they have nothing to fear and will not be afflicted.*" [18]

For all that, Mohammed by no means ceased to call on Jews and Christians to follow him, but he continued to use only persuasion.[19] Although he was in a stronger position than they, Mohammed declined the use of coercion. Surah (chapter) II, the first of the chapters dating from this period, contains one of the finest sayings of the Koran: "There is no coercion in religion; by itself, truth is enough to distinguish it from error." [20]

At the same time his controversy with the Jews became more heated. This animosity toward the Jews was but an understandable reaction against the opposition which the Jews were already mounting to his national hegemony. Mohammed then began to organize his new religion, borrowing most of the outward structure from Jewish and Christian practices and from old Arab customs.

---

[18] *Koran* II, 59; V, 73. These statements obviously do not please the commentators of the Koran, who unanimously maintain that these two verses are abrogated by *Koran* III, 79; "He who follows another religion than Islam follows a religion that is unacceptable, and in the next world he will be counted among the number of the lost."

[19] *Koran* II, 38, 41. 45.

[20] *Koran* II, 257.

The Return to Mecca

At this time Mohammed was involved in a struggle to the end with the tribe of Quraysh and the idolaters of Arabia. After an absence of eight years at Medina the prophet was able to reenter Mecca on January 11, 630 as the undoubted leader, without striking a blow. He then became more and more intolerant toward idolaters. For them Islam became practically compulsory. The same period also saw the beginning of violence being used with regard to the Jews. Raids were also organized against Christian tribes that yielded and paid tribute.

However, all things considered, these raids can hardly be called a religious persecution in the strict sense of the word. Mohammed still accepted the existence of the "people of the scripture" alongside of Islam and subject to it. If he fought them on occasion, it was like any other national leader who meets with obstacles or, quite simply, is aware of his superior strength. But he never excited his followers to fight Jews or Christians *as such*. In order to deny this, the commentators of the Koran interpreted the threats exclusively addressed to *idolaters* in such a way as to cover Jews and Christians: "Fight for Allah against those that fight against you. . . . Kill them wherever you find them. . . . Fight them till there is no perversion left and all religion is Allah's."[21] "When you meet unbelievers, hit them on the neck."[22]

The true attitude of Mohammed toward non-Moslems may be summed up by verse 29 of Surah IX: "Fight those that do not believe in Allah or in the last day and who do not consider forbidden what Allah and his apostle have declared as such and who do not profess the true religion among those who have received the book until they humbly pay tribute with their own hands."

Mohammed's Final Position

In the light of these texts we may sum up Mohammed's final position with regard to non-Moslems in the following points:

[21] *Koran* II, 186-9; VIII, 40.
[22] *Koran* XLVII, 4; IX, 5. 13.

(a) As a political group founded on the common basis of religion Islam must strive to subject to its hegemony all other groups that do not accept its faith by imposing a treaty of alliance and some form of contribution, called *gizya* (tribute or capitulation).

(b) As a faith, Islam is the only wholly true religion.

(c) Idolaters have no religion. If they are Arabs they must be forced by every means to embrace Islam. Mohammed did not consider the case of non-Arab idolaters. At the time of the Moslem conquests outside the Arab peninsula, the same rule was applied when possible.

(d) Insofar as the "people of the book" are concerned, they have a religion which in itself remains true because it was revealed by Allah; if this religion does not completely agree with Islam it is because they have falsified it in order to follow their lusts and because they refuse to admit the improvements to *the* one religion made by Mohammed by Allah's order: this makes their religion a religion apart. They must be fought not because of their religion but in order to bring them to submit themselves to Islam which alone must have the hegemony, at least in Arabia.

(e) Since religion is the sole foundation of the nation, or rather since religion and nation are one and the same, Jews, Christians and Sabaeans have their own respective nations alongside of the Moslem nation and subject to it. As long as they observe the treaty which binds them to Islam and pay their tribute regularly, they must not be molested. In other words, Islam as a religious nation has, within the same territory, the same position with regard to the Christian or Jewish nation which a sovereign nation would have with regard to a subject nation in another territory.

What Are the Problems Today?

Since they want to reconcile this teaching of the Koran with the requirements of modern democratic regimes, the Moslem States are faced with more than one delicate problem.

1. First of all, there is the problem of free choice of religion.

Today no one is forced to embrace Islam, even among the "idolaters". But if a Christian or Jew is free to become a Moslem, a Moslem is not free to become Christian or Jew. Such a conversion used to be punishable by death. Moreover, the convert is subjected to all kinds of threats and social pressures.

2. The logical result of this is that Islam forbids all missionary activity or evangelization that tends to turn Moslems away from their religion. The problem is complicated by the fact that, rightly or wrongly, "mission" is confused with "colonialism". The fight against imperialism implies a fight against the mission.

3. Christianity and Judaism are not forbidden but they are tolerated rather than accepted. In any case, there is no question of an equality between them and Islam. Islam remains *the* religion; Judaism and Christianity are beliefs that are "protected" on condition that they are subjected. Their adherents are *dhimmis,* i.e., tributaries with limited rights. Of course, the constitutions of modern Moslem States all recognize full equality of rights for all citizens without religious distinction, but this recognition in theory leaves room in practice for all kinds of religious discrimination according to the numerical importance of the Christian population and the democratic evolution attained by each State.

4. Most Moslem States are still bent on proclaiming Islam as the religion of the State. This does not necessarily cause religious discrimination with regard to the non-Moslems, but these latter may well fear that this will lead to a legalized return to their condition of being "protected and subjected", the condition they were subject to before modern freedom appeared on the scene.

At the start Islam presented a teaching which was relatively more liberal than that of the contemporary Christian empires of East and West, though not more liberal than the Christianity of the Gospels. Today States with a Christian majority have cast off the restrictive theories of the Middle Ages. Having rediscovered Christ's teaching in its original purity, the Church is in no way hampered by this liberal tendency of our age. In order to keep up with this movement the Moslem States are faced with the hard choice of either going beyond the teaching of Islam or greatly modifying it. One can understand that their development cannot be as speedy as one would wish it.

Jacques Vroemen/*Nijmegen, Netherlands*

Religious Freedom in Newly Independent African States

I am under the impression that the term "religious freedom" is commonly restricted to its juridical sense, referring either to relations between the Church and the State or the individual and the State. But I for one would like to see us reassess the term and make it more generally applicable. Thus we might well include the religious freedom of an individual or a group to preach a particular religion to others or, for that matter, the freedom to profess any faith and confess it publicly. Although this does not necessarily imply an *essential* difference of meaning, within a political context it often tends in this direction. In addition to the relations between Church (or Churches) and State, we might inquire, for instance, just how far the Church (understood as the "hierarchy") will allow the individual believer to interpret its official message on the basis of his own insights and conscience. We could even go further and distinguish between strictly religious actions, such as rites and celebrations, and religious activity within the "secular" domain, where not only the Church, but other institutions as well, particularly the State, have their own natural interests.

To deal with every one of these considerations is beyond the scope of my present article. However, there are two aspects of religious freedom which clearly belong together, at least where Africa is concerned. I am referring to the relationship between

Church and State and between the indigenous Church and the foreign Church. Although my particular emphasis will be addressed to the Church-State relationship, I would like my readers to bear both aspects in mind.

The Constitutional Position

Upon reviewing the Constitutions of the new African States,[1] their similarity is readily noticed. This is partly the result of the rapid process of unification afoot in the world today even in the area of law, and partly due to the general similarity among the Constitutions of the colonialist States which served the African lawmakers as models. Consequently, all of the African States have ratified the *Universal Declaration of the Rights of Man* (1948) which also recognizes the rights guaranteeing religious freedom. However, the Constitutions tend to differ regarding the particular application of these rights. Most States have declared their intention to be democratic, socialist and *neutral regarding religion,* and they refuse to tolerate discrimination because of race, sex, language or *religion.* A few States, while recognizing freedom of religion, do profess a "State religion". This is particularly true of the northern Arab States which officially recognize Islamism, but we would like to exclude them from our present discussion. This also occurs in a few States that have a very ancient religious (non-Islamic) tradition of their own, such as Ethiopia and Burundi where the persons of the emperor and the *mwami* are regarded as sacred and inviolable respectively. Here it is a question of an autochthonic African phenomenon, namely, the institution of a sacred kingship, coupled with a view of the world in which the natural order and the course of natural events are considered to reflect the supernatural order. I mention this to show that it is not due to Christian influence alone that a number of States, such as Lybia, Madagascar, Ruanda and Burundi, explicitly recognize God as creator in their respective Constitutions.

[1] M. Raë, *Les perspectives de la démocratie en Afrique* (Brussels, 1964).

All African States, while recognizing religious freedom, maintain that it should not conflict with the general welfare, public order or "good morals". In this regard there is complete harmony between Church and State, since the conciliar *Declaration on Religious Freedom* admits these limitations (Ch. I, nn. 3, 4, 7 and passim).[2] Therefore, all States recognize the right to religious freedom, and some even formulate it in very positive terms.

The Situation in Actual Practice

All this leads logically to the question of how this religious freedom fares in practice. Most governments show great appreciation of the missions and Churches; this is probably not unconnected with the fact that most African leaders and politicians received their education from foreign missionaries. In general there is no interference with worship. Although we sometimes receive the impression that there is less freedom in the new States than there was during the colonial period, this is only because they want a decisive voice in forming their own national policy. Consequently, they demand an overall control in those areas where the foreign missions had been traditionally active, but which are, nevertheless, primarily the concern of the State, such as education and health. A similar impression is sometimes created by the fact that some missionaries have had to make the painful discovery that independence has diminished their political and social status within the community. Another not irrelevant factor is that African officials occasionally like to impress people with their new functions. But most missionaries, on being questioned, say that they are left completely free to perform their religious duties, and they recognize the necessity of political independence if Africa is to enjoy full emancipation.

Even in so-called Communist-orientated countries, religion receives its due recognition. Ex-presidents such as Nkrumah of Ghana and Dacko of the Central African Republic, who were

[2] Vatican Council II, *Declaration on Religious Freedom* (C.T.S. of Ireland), pp. 5-7. 9.

deposed, among other reasons, on account of their relations with China, showed a great appreciation for the work of the Church. In spite of his conflict with the Church, Nkrumah supported it. Where Africa is concerned, one should very much beware of regarding relations with Communist countries as synonymous with anti-religious feelings.

The Church is also free in Africa to voice its warnings against corruption and abuse of power, as happened, for example, at the regional episcopal conference of Yacendé (Cameroon) in June, 1964. It can even do this in Rhodesia and South Africa, but I shall return to this point.

Traditionally the Churches have had close ties with education, since in the past this was the main means of disseminating their teachings. Even today they retain control of more than half the educational facilities in most African countries, and in one case, more than 90 percent. Because of the tendency toward nationalization and equalization of State and private education, it is of some importance to know just how much religious instruction remains possible in the schools. According to reports given at the Pan-African Conference on Catholic education at Leopold-ville in August, 1965, the *droit d'entrée* (the right to give religious instruction in the schools) is generally granted for secondary schools within the represented African States. As far as primary education is concerned, of the 23 countries that made reports on the matter, 9 admitted that religious instruction was part of the syllabus; of the remaining 14, only 8 reported that religious teachers could freely enter the school, while in the remaining 6 countries this was forbidden.[3]

The Conference found this right of entry unsatisfactory, since the practice did not leave enough opportunity for Catholic formation, and in so doing the Conference emphasized its preference for Catholic schools. On this point, in East Africa particularly, there is a tendency, apart from nationalization, to treat State and private education in one and the same manner. This

[3] "Conférence Panafricaine de l'Enseignement Catholique" (Leopold-ville: August, 1965), in *Vivante Afrique* 242 (Jan.-Feb. 1966).

means that private education is also eligible for State subsidy. A healthy cooperation between State and Church is developing there.

Against this generally auspicious background a few adverse cases stand out in relief. In the Sudan, the pressure of Islamic expansion from the North weighs heavily on the non-Arab-dominated and widely Christianized South. Foreign missionaries are regarded as rebel supporters and have for the most part been exiled. In this instance, the Church has become the victim of ethnic conflict.

In Congo-Brazzaville the political one-party system with its particular ideology precipitated a collision between Church and State. The insistence on unification in countries where there is a serious vacuum in authority, organization and development seems a practical necessity for the time being. When Christian organizations refused to support this nationalistic movement, the Church fell into discredit. But here the contact between the Church and the government has certainly not yet been severed. The Church will simply have to reexamine her traditional structure in this area.[4]

In South Africa the Churches maintain a somewhat dubious position regarding race relations. The most important and most traditional Protestant Church there, the Dutch Reformed Church, is, from the historical point of view, really one of the main props of the apartheid ideology. There are almost 2,000 separate African Churches in the Union of South Africa, and until recently they were satisfied with rather general protests against apartheid discrimination. In a situation where it is desperately difficult to find an alternative, this frequently causes unnecessary resentment. Some Churches, and occasionally even a Catholic one, actually support apartheid. In recent years, however, there have been a few hopeful interracial contacts of an interdenominational nature, despite the obstructionist tactics of the government.

[4] Recently the schools have been nationalized here. This is wholly in accordance with the radical course which this government pursues.

In the Portuguese territories discrimination is more social and political than racial. In the domain of social and economic development the missions cooperate with the government, but tensions remain with regard to ecclesiastical and political matters. Historically, the difficulties can be traced to the 14th century when Rome made a treaty with the king of Portugal, granting him the right to all territories "discovered" by the Portuguese, on condition that he then spread the faith there. Although the Pope limited this right of patronage in 1622, certain ecclesiastical rights in the "overseas territories" have again been included in a treaty with Salazar, and this seriously hampers the Church's freedom to speak out on the issue between Portugal and the Africans. Once independence is achieved, the Church there, more than anywhere else, will feel the burden of having taken sides with Western imperialism.

In Gabon, where the president has been restored to power with the help of French troops after an unsuccessful attempt to dislodge him, the Church is looked upon as an opponent because it disapproved his revengeful countermeasures. Tension is also growing in Rhodesia, where the Church now openly supports the rights of the African majority.

Conclusion

The instances I have cited show that the Church's situation in those African territories still dominated by whites differs from that prevailing in States which have attained their independence. In the white-dominated areas the Church is becoming increasingly outspoken in its defense of the African majority, but its attempt at moderation has incurred criticism from both sides. In the "moderate" African States (particularly the former French colonies), which still have close ties with the West, people are less critical toward the Church than they are in the "radical" States (Ghana and Guinea, to mention only two), where it is held under tight surveillance by the State. Both these blocs are subject to ever increasing State control. The growing complexity of life and the need for socialization encourage State intervention throughout the world. But in Africa there is the additional need to create new nations out of a multiplicity of groups that differ widely in historical background and economic status.

The Churches have to recognize that, in spite of all the good they have done, they have been a source of division. Africa is rightly afraid of foreign intervention. Since everything turns on unity, the Churches might well ask themselves whether it is reasonable to maintain Christian organizations alongside similar government organizations. Certainly, in what may be called semi-ecclesiastical activities, particularly in development programs of every kind, they will have to integrate their activities with State projects. Their own interests in these areas should constitute their main concern. They should also examine whether the presence of a foreign Church in Africa should not primarily express itself within the general effort toward development, although inspired, certainly, by Christian principles. Control, organization and strictly religious functions (sacraments, liturgy, preaching) should be handed over with increasing rapidity to the indigenous clergy. These, in turn, should as far as possible be trained within their own culture, and not within a Latin-European microcosm as was formerly the case. In time, this might dispel the suspicions of some African governments that remember all too well the Christian Churches' historic ties with the West's overall economic and spiritual imperialism in Africa.

Joseph Masson, S.J./*Rome, Italy*

Religious Freedom in the Light of Hinduism

N ow that Vatican Council II has accepted a text on religious freedom after a lively debate, it might be profitable to compare the ideas contained in this document with the Hindu approach. It might seem obvious that the best way to proceed would be to compare Christian and Hindu ideas point by point in detail, but such a method is unfortunately impossible for various reasons. Yet, the study of these reasons—with which I shall begin—is in itself already extremely enlightening; every time we see that there is a certain incompatibility we begin to understand a little more about the Hindu approach.

Difference in Conditions and in the Manner
of Posing the Problem

1. The fact which prevents us from proceeding at once, and perhaps forever, with a comparison between the Hindu solution and the Christian one is, first of all, an external and general reason, namely, *a different religious situation,* a different way of presenting and putting into practice any problem and any solution whatever.

Catholicism is a religion with a hierarchical structure and the system of its beliefs is clearly marked off by its formulations. No doubt, not everything is defined. The conciliar debate has shown that there are considerable differences of opinion, especially on the point we are discussing. Even after the promulgation not everything has been decided, or even made clear. But on this point, as on all the others, we have a *text* which stands *on its own* and is *authoritative*. Numerous scholars will explore it systematically and may arrive at a common exegesis through their studies and various meetings which keep them in contact with a supreme and permanent authority.

Hinduism has nothing of the sort. It has no dogmatic authority that is universally established and accepted. There are only groups of scholars, somewhat rare and rather limited, whose opinions swing from the narrowest kind of traditionalism to the broadest modernism. It "lives itself out" without trying hard to define itself. Their practical attitudes, moreover, vary as much as their basic approach. One has but to think of the differences among Tagore, Gandhi, Nehru, Ramakrishna and Radhakrishnan. Hinduism does not even want to define itself.[1] Therefore, one would have to either examine the "live" case of each of these great religious men, which is obviously impossible here, or try, after such a study, to suggest some main features that may constitute a common "image". This latter is what I shall try to do.

Even then, this common image must not aim at a solution of the problem but, without going so far, aim at suggesting how the problem should be put, or better still, aim at getting at the basic axioms that underlie the question and condition the answer.

2. Therefore, we hope to discover *an internal and specific motive, a group of basic presuppositions* which prevent the parallel comparison which we would have liked to make. Indeed, one could really "compare" the solutions if we could formulate the same problem in the same terms and with the same assumptions. But, considered in depth, these assumptions cannot be reconciled, and I want to show this from various points of view.

(a) The *first* and basic *Christian assumption* in the problem

---

[1] "Hinduism has come to be a tapestry of the most variegated tissues and almost endless diversity of hues" (S. Radhakrishnan, *A Hindu View of Life,* p. 20).

of freedom—and in any religious problem, for that matter—is that there exists an *objective multiplicity of objective beings,* or, at the heart of our problem, that there exist human persons (in the plural) and *one* ultimate person. Moreover, these beings are objectively *distinct* from one another without being isolated from one another.

But this first basic assumption is countered at once by a *first objection on the part of the Hindu* which is just as basic. On the highest level of Hinduism there exists only one substantial reality, which is permanent and authentic in the most intense sense of the word. The supposition that there are many men who hesitate about several authentic religious systems that are objectively distinct and even different, as if they were faced with a choice between a supreme and final "this *or* that?", can only come about for the Hindu because one starts from a first, unwarranted preconception, namely, the absolutization of what is multiple, temporal, relative and merely apparent. The whole Hindu tradition protests against this absolutization, beginning with the ancient Upanishads more than 500 years before Christ.[2] Therefore, one is faced with a dilemma: there is an ultimate and unique reality existing in an absolute situation (but then it is alone and the hypothesis of a choice in a pure illusion [*mâyâ*], or we are still caught up in multiple appearances (but then none of those fluid and provisional things can present itself to us with the claims of an absolute).

(b) Christianity rests on a *second assumption*. It maintains that certain *formulations* (dogmatic, ritual or even parabolical) have an *objective value* in the way they present the ultimate which we have to choose. These express, analogically but validly

[2] At the beginning *was* the Being, alone and without second (*Chandegya-Upanishad,* 6, 2, 1). This Brahma *is* all. By recognizing in this Brahma the beginning, end and present of all, one is in peace (*ibid.,* 3, 14, 1). Containing all actions, all desires and the totality of the world without expression and without anxiety, this Atman in my heart is the Brahma itself (*ibid.,* 3, 14, 4). Whoever *considers as separate* the various "actions" (i.e., manifestations in their multiplicity) of the Brahma does not know him (*Brhad-Aranyaka Upanishad,* 1, 4, 7) and *cannot* know him.

by means of corrective statements (*via negationis, affirmationis eminentiae,* etc.), the nature of religious realities, either in themselves or in their mutual relationship, as capable of existing together, or as mutually exclusive, or in their relevance for us, and so they are "true" or "false" in themselves (e.g., God or idol) and in their saving relevance for us.

But the Hindu would immediately reply that a formulated expression is essentially inadequate for the transmission of any reality insofar as it is experienced, and still more for the transmission by proposition of the ultimate reality which cannot be measured by what is finite. And so, no definite formula of any religious system can either meet the concreteness of the religious ultimate or transmit it in its entirety. More than that, such a formulation is essentially vitiated by the subjective character and limitations of the one who proclaims it. How then could the basic dilemma about the ultimate choice (which the conciliar Declaration presupposes) possibly relate, absolutely and totally, to "formulas of belief" or "practical systems", none of which can claim to be a faithful, exhaustive and definitive presentation?[3] The most one could say would be that one of these systems might appear preferable to *me* for the *moment.*

(c) *A third Christian assumption* follows from the second. The man who seeks is supposed to be able to *see sufficiently,* while within the domain of what is finite and provisional, that there is an Infinite of an ultimate and total character, and to see this in such a way that he can take up an absolute position with regard to this infinite. The creator is revealed in the creature (this is the objective order). The creator can be found there through the conscience, whether before or after the coming of Christ (this is the subjective order) in such a way that an attentive and faithful man can reach certain conclusions (the proofs of the existence of God, the credibility of the revelation, etc.). As Claudel put it, for the Christian the creature is an "allusion"

[3] This Atman is smaller than a grain of rice, of birdseed, even than a kernel of a birdseed; and this Atman is greater than the atmosphere, the vault of heaven, and all the worlds" (*Chandogya-Upanishad,* 3, 14, 3).

to God; it can even be the direct expression of God (in Jesus Christ, God made *man*).

The Hindu, again, sees here a basic difficulty. For him every creature is an "illusion", to pursue Claudel's way of putting it.[4] Through the concept and even through ordinary existential experience, objectively manifold and logically discursive, we can never perceive what is beyond reason, the unique, that is "totally Other". No man who has the true knowledge (*Vidya*) of the true state of reality can ever "see" a "system", because this system cannot be a revealed image of the ineffable, full and faithful enough in me to demand the total assent of my whole concrete being. This is the homage which true freedom would only offer to the supreme being truly made manifest and recognized as such.

(d) There is a *fourth Christian assumption* which I have deliberately introduced into the previous sentence: the affirmation and a certain conception of freedom. For Christianity, man is a creature that is free by nature and is, moreover, supernaturally freed from sin in that "freedom in which Christ has set us free". This basic condition of a liberty, which he possesses by nature and a supernatural liberation which is possible, allows a man to reverse the basic choice of his life (*metanoia*). He has to do it once he sees his basic error: "Who are you, Lord?" "I am Jesus whom you persecute; arise and go into the town; there *they will tell you* what you must do" (Acts 9, 4). A freedom, a demand made from outside, an overriding inner duty, the discharge of which will determine a whole destiny, to be separated for the sake of the Gospel—all this is the absolute and final option which Saul had to face.

[4] Here one can only deny all positive statements and say that it is "not like this". Its name (i.e., its deepest nature) is the real of the real (i.e., the supreme real); after having achieved the knowledge of this fact, the only formula left is "Neti, neti" (*Brhad-Aranyaka Upanishad* 2, 3, 6; 3, 9, 26, etc.). One can compare this with Tagore: "All that I feel about religion is from vision and not from knowledge" (*The Religion of Man*, p. 107), or Schlipp, *The Philosophy of S. Radhakrishnan*, p. 9, where there is a mention of the "undogmatic apprehensions which Hinduism provides". Gandhi said: "There is but one tree, but many branches. . . . We know no more about pure religion than we know about God."

But while the Hindu may admire the courage and greatness of these "final and total options", he would consider them as mistaken, particularly if they are not even preceded by Saul's lightning-like experience. For the Hindu, man is essentially a being that is the consequence of something else and always on the move.[5] He comes into being through a succession of existences, each of which is the fruit and the reward of previous good or bad existences. This is the law of the endless *karma*. Perfection consists in submitting yourself to it; it is never a question of "breaking with" it but of "admitting" it and of following the course of things according to the moral and cosmic order prevailing in each existence. These "things" include the religion in which one is born. This birth in a given religion is "part of the order"—and it is an "order" in every sense of the word—which must be respected. The Hindu cannot do better than remain Hindu. Conversion would be to go against the order of nature, a rebellion against justice. The Buddhist or Christian must act in the same way. Their problem, if correctly put in fairness and in justice, will never be: "Must I change my religion?", but "Must I change my way of life in the religion where I am?" It would be just as strange to query one's belonging to one's own religion as to query one's belonging to one's family, one's caste or even one's blood group.[6]

And so, the orthodox Hindu would consider it equally irregular, unhealthy and heterodox to try to make others abandon the religion in which they are born and choose another one. Gandhi did not merely object to the supposed dishonesty of Christian "proselytism"; he objected above all, and much more deeply, to the "disorder", the social and religious "sin" of violating the world's order (*rta*) and the laws (*dharma*) of universal justice. To change religion is to refuse to keep one's place in the "mystery" of the total reality. It is not freedom, but blind anarchy.

(e) This leads to the *fifth Christian assumption*. Without de-

[5] "What is built forever is *forever building*" (Radhakrishnan, *A Hindu View of Life*, p. 21).

[6] Gandhi once used this rather familiar but very significant expression: "For me, Hinduism is like my wife: she is not perfect but she is mine."

nying that man is an "intersubjective" being and that his self-existence is for a large part an existence involved in others, Christianity maintains that the concrete unit in this mosaic of situations and relations on this earth is the individualized conscious and free person. Whatever options man takes, each finds the supreme tribunal in his own conscience and the supreme law in "the law of God written in his heart". No authority can impose itself from outside on a sincere man who has sought the light as far as lies within him, naturally also taking account of his environment. He takes his decision before God and is only answerable for it to God. No society, apart from one in which he would have recognized the presence of God's infallible light, can impose its views on him. His own serious conviction and his faith are the norms which guide him.

The Hindu would not deny the ultimate value of one's experience and one's personal religious attitude—far from it—but he would find it far more difficult to recognize these in a possible break with the environment. If, for the Hindu, the religious choice is essentially individual and experimental, it is also "co-experimental", so to speak—that is, it lies in a religious experience which is *lived with* the rest of the environment. The Hindu sees his religious choice as made, emphatically, by a being that exists "with" and "in" and "for". This is not only true of the old tradition, now left behind, by which a woman had to live with (and dependently on) her father, then her husband and then her eldest son, and to look upon them as her *deva* and the type of her whole religious life. It is still true and in line with the whole classical tradition of religious search and training that a Hindu who "seeks God" does not join a "system" but submits himself to a wise *guru* (one might almost say, whatever his teaching) in order to live a combined religious experience with him and under him, attaching little importance to the way it is expressed as long as it respects and fits in with the broad stream of a thousand currents of all those Hindus who sought the ultimate.[7]

---

[7] The texts used by the "teachers" are significant in themselves. They

Some Similarities and Some Immediate Solutions

Does it now follow from all these contrasts between Christianity and Hinduism that they have nothing but axioms, problems and solutions that are irreconcilable? That would be rather exaggerating the situation.

However monistic, spiritualist and relativist classical Hinduism may be, it has to live. In any case, a number of Indian systems did not yield to this monistic triumph without fierce struggles. A dualism which affirmed, with the existence of the Spirit, the existence of at least a certain kind of matter flourished in the past in the Sankhya. This is in itself and everywhere a perpetual temptation for the strange complex creatures we are. So is it also in India.

The greatest of the Hindu monists, Shankara, has had to compromise with the "common experience" and the "problems of the manifold". In reality as in truth, he distinguished two orders: the supreme order where the real is unique, the way experience, the end identity and basically unlimited and ineffable religion. Then he accepted the pragmatic order (*vyavaharika*) where the real is manifold, the "ways" vary, the end is still a distinction and "religions" are both expressible and limited in their formulation. This second order is provisional and, with regard to the first order, illusory. Nevertheless, on this "hypothetical" level of ordinary experience, everything happens "as if" things were real, distinct, related, ordered and according to laws that ensure their harmony and survival. Man can therefore express, specify and promulgate these laws, principles and provisions and propose various forms, various ways and various religions. We take these as real and firm, while the Hindu will see them as provisional and frail, but at least we can discuss them together, and the more so since India in practice has clearly come closer to what are called "Western" views, the root of which, however, is Christian.

In this practical order the demands of orthodoxy in modern Hinduism are varied. One of the best known and no doubt fairest

---

are anxious to maintain the living contact and often begin with *evam kutam* (this is what has been said), and then give a quotation.

expressions is a kind of creed which Gandhi once put out and which contains six articles: belief in the sacred writings; belief in the *avatars* of the gods; the lawfulness of venerating images; the reincarnation of living beings; the division of men into castes, and the respect for the cow (*Young India,* 1921).

Even so, Gandhi interpreted these beliefs in a much more supple way than conservative Hinduism. One might perhaps interpret Gandhi's credo as a basic *option* with regard to the ultimate as unique (particularly as revealed by the Upanishads), accompanied on the practical level by *three judgments* on the usefulness of a definite relationship with the superhuman (the gods), the human (the collective society of mankind) and the subhuman (the cow as symbol and epitome of "all the rest" seen as beneficent).

When these demands are taken for granted—and sometimes less than these[8]—we can look at the Hindu view of *religious liberty*.

(a) Within the enduring Hinduism (*sanatanadharma*), so accommodating metaphysically and methodologically, almost all systems can coexist: both the monistic Vedanta and the dualist Shankya are orthodox. The worship of Vishnu—in his manifold forms and names—and of Siva, including their wives, families and a number of other deities, are all equally lawful, though not all practiced to the same degree. There are at least three main ways of salvation, and all three are respected in the best known and most highly valued of Hindu scriptures, the *Bhagavadgita*. It knows self-discipline and ascetic activity (*karman*), the ardent and total devotion to a chosen deity (*bhakti*) and the contemplative gnosis (*jñana*). All this coexists and often merges according to period, region or group. India has had its fanatics, since these appear everywhere, but within itself Hinduism is definitely not fanatical; it shows an inexhaustible—and logical—comprehension for the immensely inventive spirit and religious diversity of its followers.

[8] Thus, an inegalitarian social institution caste is ignored (if not condemned) in the Constitution, but it continues to exist in a rather large measure.

(b) *Toward other religions,* particularly dogmatic ones whose basic ideas are radically opposed to its own, Hinduism is on the defensive. It meets Christian or Moslem "fanaticism" with the certainty that its supple relativist position is invincible and will triumph in the end. It believes in, and works for, the ultimate unity of all religions in respectful and friendly coexistence of differences which may even be contradictory. It expects no good from dogmatism. The present president wrote: "The belief in monopolies of religious truth has often led to pride, fanaticism and conflict." [9] That is why, at the end of 1965, he insisted, as a Hindu, on assisting at the welcome of a Christian Eucharistic Congress at Bombay and, within two days, taking part in a World Congress of Buddhism at Sarnath. One cannot blame India for preaching peaceful coexistence, even in religion, when one re- members the violent conflicts between Hindus and Moslems that have occurred more than once during the last twenty years.

Hinduism is tolerant with regard to any opinion that does not pretend to be absolute; it is basically intolerant toward those religions that claim the absolute truth and that are therefore necessarily "intolerant" toward any opposite truth.[10]

Insofar as "proselytism" is concerned—that is, any kind of missionary activity—the Hindu attitude varies according to the level, the place and the time.

Article 17 of the Constitution, which was debated thoroughly and worked out most carefully, recognizes explicitly the right "to profess, practice and propagate" a religion. Later legislation maintained, in opposition to certain restrictive interpretations of this article, that this right was granted not only to the citizens

[9] Cf. Schlipp, *The Philosophy of Radhakrishnan,* p. 72. Gandhi said: "Men are not bricks that you can take from one place to another." And again: "Are we sure that we know more about the truth than those people? . . . I am not trying to give my religion to another" (cf. Mirabehn, *Gleanings,* June, 1942). Or again: "God is personal for those who need his personal presence. He is incarnate for those that need contact with him" (*Young India,* March 19, 1931).

[10] There are two articles on this: A. Huart, "Hindouisme et Tolérance Religieuse," in *Nouvelle Rev. Théol.* (1936), pp. 834-52; M. Queguiner, "Intolérance hindoue et Tolérance indienne," in *Etudes* 290 (1956), pp. 161-76.

but to any person peacefully residing in India and behaving according to its laws.

In actual fact, Christian missionary activity, which is often charitable, social and educational, depends on the supreme arbiter in such matters, and this is not the central government but the government of each State for its own territory. The attitude of these governments may vary. In strongly Hindu districts and where the governing class is strongly Hindu, the tolerance in principle may degenerate into a war, hot or cold. Hence, there have been such incidents as refusals of visas and expulsion of missionaries, while Catholic priests have been brought to court for manipulating conversions through economic or psychological pressure. The Nyogi Report, which dealt with this subject, was prohibited by the late Pandit Nehru.

At the moment the situation is more relaxed. This may have been the effect of the Eucharistic Congress of Bombay and especially the Pope's visit to India. It may also have been influenced by the struggle against materialist communism, as this showed the need for maintaining the primacy of the spiritual in freedom. On a deeper level, it may also have been a side effect of the lay mentality which wants a separation of "Church and State", a mentality that is more and more accepted by educated Indians.[11]

It is true that one cannot say that Christianity and Hinduism agree on the *principles* that underlie a study of religious liberty. At least they both have reached some immediate and practical conclusions that are comparable and even show a certain *approchement*. One can only hope that these conclusions will be applied permanently and universally. "The Church severely forbids anyone to force another to embrace the faith or to lure him to it by unsuitable means; by the same token she asks that nobody be turned away from his faith by iniquitous vexations." [12]

[11] It is interesting that the subcommission of UNESCO, which has devoted years to the study of a declaration on religious liberty, is presided over by an Indian. This group works and can only work on the basis of equality of religions and what in practice is required by human dignity and current legal practice.

[12] Cf. the *Decree on the Church's Missionary Activity* which clearly refers to the *Declaration on Religious Freedom*, nn. 2, 4 and 10.

Teodoro Jiménez-Urresti/*Bilbao, Spain*

Religious Freedom in a Catholic Country: The Case of Spain

I

PRINCIPLES

The *Declaration on Religious Freedom* notes that "religious freedom . . . has to do with immunity from coercion in civil society [in religious affairs]. Therefore, it leaves untouched traditional Catholic doctrine on the *moral duty of men and societies* toward the true religion and toward the one Church of Christ" (1e).* The Council here defines the duty of men and societies and shows a parallel analogy between the duties of men on the one hand and societies on the other toward objective truth and true religion.

It is true that the Declaration starts with a direct statement about personal values, and from a personal point of view it frequently declares that "every man has the duty, and therefore the right to seek the truth. . . ." (3a, etc.), that this truth is "the divine law—eternal, objective and universal" (3a), and that "this one true religion subsists in the Catholic and Apostolic Church" (1d). But it also states—although with less emphasis, since they do not form part of its main concern—the rights of the Church vis-à-vis political society. It does this no less clearly, emphasizing the rights due from the public authorities in society.

* References are to numbered sections and paragraphs in *The Documents of Vatican II* (N.Y.: Herder and Herder, 1966).

91

These rights have two bases: supernatural—"as a spiritual authority, established by Christ the Lord"—and natural—"as a society of men who have the right to live in society in accordance with the precepts of Christian faith" (13b). On these two bases depend the duties of the public authorities and civic society toward the Church.

The subjective norm, being a *mediate* norm of conduct, needs to be subjectivized and made immediate by conscience. This is the classic and universal principle of morality. "Man perceives and acknowledges the imperative of the divine law *through the mediation of conscience*" (3c) and must do so in such a way that "he may with prudence form for himself right and true judgments of conscience" (3a) which will become the immediate norms of his conduct (cf. 3c).

Political society or the State also has its conscience, the collective conscience of its people, which has its ultimate expression in the legal code. Therefore, the Council recognizes that there can be "*peculiar circumstances* obtaining among certain peoples", in which "special legal recognition is given in the constitutional order of society to one religious body" (6c).

From this it follows that just as man "is not to be forced to act in a manner contrary to his conscience; nor, on the other hand, is he to be restrained from acting in accordance with his conscience" (3c), the State should not be forced to act against its collective conscience or be restrained from acting in accordance with its collective conscience. Moreover, since "this Vatican Synod declares that the human person has a right to religious freedom" (2a), it also implicity recognizes that the State has the same right when it admits that the State can give special recognition to one religious body (6c), and when it states that "Government, therefore, ought indeed to take account of the religious life of the people and show it favor" (3e). Finally, if the right of the human person to religious freedom "is to be recognized in the constitutional law whereby society is governed" (2b; cf. 13c), the right of a State to religious freedom should equally be recognized in international law, since this right is founded, like that of the person, not in subjective disposition but in the "very nature" of the person, and thus of the State (2c). Parallels could be multiplied but the principle is evident.[1]

However, it must be remembered that the Council, in speaking of special circumstances (that is, the collective conscience), does say that if special recognition is given to one religious body, "it is at the same time imperative that the right of all citizens and religious bodies to religious freedom should be recognized and made effective in practice" (6c).

This special recognition in law, or constitutional recognition, implies that the civil power, the State (*potestas civilis*, in 6b) and the law (*juridica ordinatio*) have a *positive* duty to favor and foster (*fovere*, in 6b) the religious life which corresponds to the collective conscience of the people and, in a special way, to create conditions favorable to it. Negatively, it implies that this recognition should not suppose any lessening of the equality of citizens before the law—that is, that there must be no discrimination among them for religious reasons (6d). Government, in those matters that involve fundamental human rights, is not to act "in an unfair spirit of partisanship" (7c).

If this is to have any practical meaning, it must be that the resultant situation of the religious body, to which special recognition is given in the constitutional order, is not the same, juridically and socially, as that of the other religious bodies in that State.

The Council distinguishes four different grades of religious freedom. The *first* is the personal freedom to lead one's own personal life. Here there must be full equality of situation and consideration before the law, since this is a basic human right. Whether the person adopts a positive or a negative attitude to religion, his world of personal activity is inviolable because this right "has its foundation in the very dignity of the human person" (2b).

---

[1] For a fuller treatment, cf. T. Jiménez-Urresti, "Especial reconocimiento constitucional a una comunidad religiosa y límites de la libertad religiosa," in *Hechos y Dichos* (Jan. 1966), pp. 19-39.

The *second* is the person's right to form religious communities and to offer communal worship, "a requirement of the social nature both of man and of religion itself" (4a; cf. 3c). From this follows the right of these communities to "order their own lives" (4b). This right poses no problems either, since it is a question precisely of each community ordering its own life and leaving the others in peace, at least as far as their direct actions are concerned.

However, the *third* grade, the freedom for these religious bodies to publicize themselves, implies a socially positive activity toward others, for the activity is of itself an activity toward others. It must, then, in itself, take more account than in any other case of the rights of others, particularly of those passive subjects toward whom their publicizing activity is directed (cf. 4d). The *fourth* grade is the right of the community to be constitutionally recognized.

Therefore, not only must the State respect the right of religious bodies to religious freedom (6c), but religious bodies themselves must respect the right of other religious bodies to religious freedom (cf. 6a). And just as a person cannot be coerced into dialogue and communication because of respect for his freedom (cf. *libera inquisitione* in 3b), so propaganda (a social means of communication or dialogue) cannot be forced on another religious body.

In Spain, the Spanish people, with their Catholic collective conscience, reject open propaganda carried out by other non-Catholic or non-Christian bodies. They publicly admit the right to personal freedom and the right of other bodies to order their own lives, even toward those who make a free approach to these other bodies, but they do not admit the right to proselytize openly.

These principles, as we shall see, are laid down in Article 6 of the Spanish Constitution (*Fuero de los Españoles*), in the genuine belief that they do not violate the rights of anyone. They are thus raised to constitutional status. This inequality in public life and in public means of communication is seen as the simple application of the people's right to peace in their collective religious life.

These are the principles behind the Spanish attitude to religious freedom, which I have tried to express in the words of the Council itself. Now let us try to see how they are worked out in the present situation of Spain.

II

THE SPANISH SITUATION

"From the religious point of view, Spain is perhaps the most homogenous country in the world." [2] Its population of nearly 32 million is Catholic, except for 30,000 Protestants and 5,000 Jews. (These 30,000 Protestants are divided into 6,000 Plymouth Brethren, 5,400 Baptist, 3,100 Free Church, 3,800 Spanish Evangelical Church, 1,000 Episcopalians, 5,200 Seventh Day Adventists, 3,500 Pentecostal Evangelical and 2,000 Independent Evangelicals. They have 425 places of worship, 320 of them churches or chapels and the remainder in private houses. About 60% are officially recognized as chapels, and 30% are tolerated. This means one church/chapel for every 93 members, or a place of worship for every 70.[3]) The situation therefore has all the inconveniences and advantages, defects and possibilities, of a Catholic "bloc" of virtually the whole population.

Article 6 of the *Fuero* (the Law of July 17, 1945) reflects the sociological situation of the country. It states: "The profession and practice of the Catholic religion, which is that of the Spanish State, will enjoy official protection. No person will be molested

[2] Hamer, "Dialogue sans polémique sur la condition des protestants en Espagne," in *Rev. Nouv.* 10 (1949), pp. 558-64.

[3] Statistics provided by the Executive Secretary for Evangelical Defense. Cf. J. Cardona, "El Protestantismo español," in Diálogo Ecuménico I (1966), p. 70; E. Guerrero and J. Alonso, *Libertad religiosa en España: Principios, hechos, problemas* (Madrid: Fe Católica, 1962), pp. 141-72; J. Maldonado, "Los cultos no católicos en el Derecho español," in *El Concordato de 1953* (Madrid: Law Faculty of the University, 1956), pp. 403-50.

on account of his religious beliefs or private practice of his worship. Religious ceremonies or external manifestations other than those of the Catholic religion will not be permitted."

Note that what is not allowed is public and open practice, and that the limits of private practice are established: it must be within "the precincts devoted to the religious confession in question". This was laid down by governmental order in Article 2 on February 23, 1948. Article 1 of another order, dated November 12, 1945, states: "Non-Catholic religious bodies may practice their religion in any part of Spanish territory, provided that they do so within their respective places of worship and without public manifestation." Therefore, the public or official worship of each religious body is not forbidden; what is forbidden is only public propaganda.

The Constitutional Background to Article 6 of the Fuero

In the Constitutions of 1808, 1812, 1817 and 1845, the Catholic faith alone was mentioned. Article 14 of the Constitution, voted, but not promulgated, in 1856, stated: ". . . but no Spaniard or foreigner may be persecuted for his religious beliefs or religious opinions unless these are manifested in public actions contrary to religion."

The Constitution of 1869, the outcome of the revolution of 1868, gave the first expression in modern Spanish law to freedom of worship. Article 21 stated: "The Spanish nation pledges itself to maintain the practice and ministers of the Catholic faith. The public or private exercise of any other faith is guaranteed to all foreigners, without any limitation other than the universal rules of morals and law. If any Spaniards should profess any other religion, the same conditions apply to them." This is a strange formulation, with its reference to Spaniards restricted to a hypothesis, but in fact the census of a few years later revealed that only some 6,000 out of a population of 17 million—that is 3.5 out of every 10,000—professed a faith other than Catholic.[4]

---

[4] L. Pérez Mier, *Iglesia y Estado nuevo* (Madrid: Fax, 1940), p. 219; J. Maldonado, *op. cit.*, p. 412.

However, it was not from this Constitution but from that of 1876 that this Article 6 was taken, almost word for word. Article 11 of this Constitution stated: "The Catholic, apostolic, Roman religion is the religion of the State. The Nation pledges itself to maintain its practice and ministers. No one will be molested on Spanish soil for his religious opinions or for the exercise of his particular religion unless the respect due to Christian morality should demand it. Public ceremonies or manifestations other than of the State religion, however, will not be permitted."

Another antecedent is found in the Concordat of 1851, Article 1, which affirmed that the Catholic faith, "to the exclusion of all others, continues to be the sole faith of the Spanish nation".[5] This Concordat was broken by the Republic of 1931, although it is no longer possible to ascertain on what actual date and by what actual action it did so. The prologue to the apostolic Motu Proprio *Hispaniarum nuntio* of April 7, 1947, reestablishing the Rota of the Nuntiature in Madrid, suggests that it was before June 21, 1932, the date on which Pius XI legally suppressed the Tribunal of the Rota on the grounds that the Republic had already broken the solemn agreement with the Holy See.[6] It established a new system in Articles 26 and 27 of its 1931 Constitution, and by its Law of Religious Confessions and Congregations of June, 1932, there was no official religion. All faiths had the equal right to practice their worship within their respective places of worship, but in each case a special governmental approval was required for external or public manifestations. The intention was to reduce the status of Catholicism, not to raise other religions to the status Catholicism had previously enjoyed. Curi-

[5] Cf. E. Piñuela, *El Concordato de 1851 y disposiciones complementarias vigentes* (Madrid: Reus, 1921); F. Suárez, "Génesis del Concordato de 1851," in *Ius Canonicum* 3 (1963), pp. 65-250; L. Pérez Mier, *op. cit.*, pp. 216-22.

[6] Cf. J. López Ortiz, "Los cien años de la vida del Concordato de 1851," in *El Concordato de 1953*, pp. 47-9; J. Ruiz Giménez, former Ambassador to the Holy See, in a speech made while Minister of Education, in *El Concordato de 1953*, pp. 435-6.

ously, this legal situation was widely hailed in many Protestant writings as "religious freedom", whereas Article 6 was described as "oppression". This law was roundly abrogated by the Law of the New State of February 2, 1939.

Article 1 of the 1851 Concordat was reestablished in the agreement between the Spanish Government and the Holy See, dated June 7, 1941, at the request of the Nuncio, Cayetano Cigognani, who was following instructions from Rome. "Until a new Concordat is concluded, the Spanish Government undertakes to carry out the dispositions contained in the first four Articles of the Concordat of 1851."

The Cardinal of Toledo, Primate of Spain and an ex-officio Counsellor of State, was a member of the Commission that drew up Article 6. Acting on instructions from Rome he insisted (even to the extent of threatening to withdraw from the Commission) on its inclusion in the Constitution. The new State, born under a Catholic aegis in 1936 and signatory to the Agreement of 1941, could not but agree. Several embassies, concerned with obtaining specific recognition for Protestant minorities, also made representations. This recognition was of course given. It was nothing new, as it figured in the Constitution of 1876, although then it had been inserted against the wishes of the Holy See and now it was in accordance with those wishes. (The Spanish Metropolitans, in their "Instruction to the Conference" of May, 1948—printed in *Ecclesia,* the official journal of the Central Secretariat of Catholic Action, "in view of the attacks to which the Spanish hierarchy has been subjected in the last few weeks"—denounced "the illegality of Protestant proselytism", and demanded "the strict observance of the law", but declared: "Two things we can affirm with absolute certainty: first, that the toleration of dissident private worship was inserted in Article 6 of the *Fuero* with regard to foreigners resident in Spain and in view of the representations made by certain non-Catholic foreign powers; second, that the final draft of Article 6 was not made— as was the case with Article 11 of the Constitution of 1876—

without discussion with the Church, but, on the contrary, after prior discussion with the Holy See." [7])

The *Fuero,* including Article 6, was declared "The Basic Law of the Nation" (constitutional law) by Article 10 of the "Law of Succession of the Head of State" which was submitted to a national referendum, accepted by 82% of the electorate and promulgated on July 26, 1947. Article 6 thus has maximum juridical force and stability.

International Difficulties

Protests against Article 6 were soon raised in various parts of the world. The "case of Spain" and the whole question of religious freedom was widely debated. The slogan "oppression of Protestants in Spain" found support in many quarters. J. Delpech published a book with this title in England and the U.S.A. in 1956, and French and German editions also appeared. Some Protestants, such as Hughey, saw Article 6 rather as an extension of the freedom allowed to Protestants, but the general demand was for open freedom.

Spain was treated to a downpour of printed propaganda, strongly anti-Catholic and not exactly ecumenical in tone, attacking even the dogmas of Catholicism most venerated in Spain —those concerning the eucharist, the Virgin Mary and the pope. It was not surprising that the Spanish bishops denounced "the illegality of Protestant proselytism".

For their part, the Spanish people realized that these proselytizing activities and propaganda campaign were not devoid of political context. At this time Spain was the object of one of the greatest international intrigues of modern times, what the *Catholic Herald* of February 10, 1950 called "the most gigantic bluff of the century". As Sr. A. Martín Artajo, the Spanish Minister of Foreign Affairs, said in the *Cortes* on December 14, 1950, the "black legend" against Spain was then being diffused to a

---

[7] *Ecclesia* 8 (1941-I), pp. 673-5; 12 (1952-I), pp. 517-9. Cf. J. Postius Sala, *El Código canónico aplicado a España* (Madrid, 1926), pp. 314-5.

fantastic extent. Spain was accused of bloody campaigns against minorities, internal strife, an inhuman penal code, constant mass executions, religious persecutions, oppression of all liberties, secret police repression, anti-regionalism and genocide. This powerful international campaign was largely inspired by one of the victorious Allied powers, the Soviet Union, which had suffered a major defeat in Spain between 1936 and 1939—where the struggle between Trotskyism and Stalinism was decided and the future heads of European communism (Togliatti, Tito, Thorez and Gomulka) were active—despite the burning and sacking of churches and convents, the murder of 6,484 priests and religious, 283 nuns and 429 seminarians.[8]

At the Conferences of San Francisco, Potsdam, Paris (1945) and London (1946), Spain was excluded from the international community; the U.N. then decided on a "diplomatic offensive" and commercial, political and diplomatic blockade; in 1949 she was excluded from the Atlantic Pact and the Western Alliance and finally, with President Truman pointing to the existence of Article 6, from the Marshall Plan.[9] As Sr. A. Martín Artajo said: "Spain has paid for her neutrality far more dearly than the Axis powers for their defeat."

Foreign press and radio, sometimes in the names of Protestant pastors, launched absurd calumnies, going to the extreme reached by *Everybody's* on Christmas Day, 1948: "Not a week goes by in Spain without some member of the Protestant Church being tortured to death." [10] These calumnies brought complaints from diplomats, particularly those of Great Britain and the U.S.A., and from the Ecumenical Council at Geneva.

In Spain, people who were then suffering poverty and hardship were humiliated by being bribed to come to non-Catholic services

[8] Cf. A. Moreno, *Historia de la Persecución religiosa en España, 1936-1939* (Madrid: BAC, 1962).

[9] Press Conference of Feb. 7, 1952; statement by the former U.S. Ambassador, Stanton Griffiths, in the *New York Times,* Feb. 9, 1952; note published in Madrid by the Office of Diplomatic Information of the Spanish Government, Feb. 12, 1952. Cf. G. Fernández de la Mora, *El nuevo Estado español 1936-1961* (Madrid, 1961), p. 74.

[10] For further examples, cf. Guerrero and Alonso, *op. cit.,* pp. 117ff.

with gifts of condensed milk, clothes and money—but no Marshall aid. The phrase "Un protestante, un dolar" was coined. Feeling ran high, and it is therefore not altogether surprising that groups of young people sometimes expressed their feelings in breaking up Protestant places of worship. The fact that it was difficult to be a Protestant in Spain at the time was not so much a result of State action but, as Sr. F. Martín Sánchez, President of the National Association of Catholic Publicists said in the Pontifical Spanish College in Rome in February 1952, "a problem of the atmosphere . . . a sort of human respect in reverse".

In intellectual circles in Spain the question of religious freedom in a Catholic State was much discussed. Foreign theologians took part in the 1949 International Conversations of San Sebastián, but no common draft of a Charter of the Rights of Man was produced, because the so-called "right to freedom of [public] propaganda" for all was definitely not admitted for a people living in religious harmony and not willing to listen to propaganda from other religions. The article of the proposed Charter discussed and rejected was somewhat gentler in tone, but this was the gist of it. The 14th Spanish Theology Week in 1954 examined the same topic and reaffirmed the Spanish attitude.[11]

The Concordat of 1953

The Spanish State and people are sometimes accused of being "more papist than the pope" for not allowing freedom of open non-Catholic propaganda. Appeals have even been made to the Holy See itself. In view of this, will there be a change in the Spanish attitude which considers itself to be a defense of religious freedom (cf. 4d and 7c)?

[11] Cf *Documentos* (the Journal of the San Sebastián Conversations), 1-2 (1949); 4 (1950); 8 (1950) and 10 (1952); M. Useros Carretero, "A propósito de la neutralidad confesional del Estado y el Concordato Español," in *Rev. Esp. Der. Canon* 9 (1954), pp. 225-39; XIV Sem. Esp. de Teol.: *Fundamentos teológicos del Derecho Publico Eclesiástico* (Madrid: C.S.I.C., 1954); A. A. Esteban Romero, "La XIV Semana española de Teología y las relaciones entre la Iglesia y el Estado," in *Lumen* 3 (Victoria, 1954), pp. 365-74.

The answer lies in the Concordat of 1953, in which, just a few days before it was due to be signed, Pius XII inserted the text of the first articles, thereby causing the numbering of the whole document to be changed at the last minute. Article 1 repeats Article 1 of the 1857 Concordat almost word for word. The actual texts are as follows:

Article 1 of the Concordat of 1851: *The Catholic, Apostolic, Roman religion, to the exclusion of all others, remains the only religion of the Spanish nation and will always be maintained* in the dominions of His Catholic Majesty, *with all the rights and prerogatives which it ought to enjoy according to the law of God and* the provisions of *the sacred canons.*

Article 3 of the Concordat of 1953: *The Catholic, Apostolic, Roman religion remains the only religion of the Spanish nation* and *will enjoy the rights and prerogatives due to it in conformity with divine law and canon law.*

The two articles are thus almost exactly alike in expression, and certainly in content, since the fact that the phrase "to the exclusion of all others" was omitted from the 1953 text was counterbalanced in a "final protocol" which "forms an integral part of the said Concordat" of 1953 and, "in conjunction with Article 1", affirms that, in regard to freedom of open expression, "the provisions of Article 6 of the *Fuero de los Españoles* will remain in force on Spanish territory".

And so, for the third time in a few years (the Agreement of 1941, the *Fuero* of 1945 and the Concordat of 1953), the Catholic religion was officially recognized, in contrast to the tendency —of which Maritain was the basic representative—toward a lay (not laicist) State. Maritain delivered a course of six lectures at the 1934 International Summer University of Santander, later published in *Humanisme intégrale,* arguing this thesis under the title "Spiritual and Temporal Problems of a New Christianity". The 1940 Portuguese Concordat supported his point of view.[12]

There are really two series of Concordats. The one in which

[12] Cf. T. Jiménez-Urresti, *Estado e Iglesia* (Vitoria, 1958) pp. 18-19, 22-4, 148-9, for reactions to Maritain and the development of his thought.

the Catholic religion is recognized as the only one of the State started with the Spanish Concordat of 1851 and was followed by those of Costa Rica and Nicaragua in 1857 and of El Salvador, Venezuela, Ecuador and Colombia, all in 1862, ending with the Italian Concordat of 1929 which, though different in other respects, admits this same principle. The other—corresponding to a different sociological situation, which is content with affirming the freedom of the Church within the juridical system of the country—started with the Napoleonic Concordat of 1801, and was followed by those of Bavaria (1817), Serbia (1914), Littonia (1922), Bavaria again in 1924, Poland (1925), Lithuania (1927), Rumania (1929), Prussia (1929), Germany (1933) and Austria (1934). If the last Concordat before the Spanish one of 1953—that of Portugal in 1940—seemed to establish the historical continuity of the second series, that Spanish Concordat of 1953, followed by that of Santo Domingo of 1954, reversed the tendency.[13] The Concordat therefore reaffirmed the former Spanish position. General Franco, ratifying the Concordat in his "Message to the Cortes" of October 24, 1953, said: "In any case, tolerance of different beliefs and practices does not mean freedom of propaganda to foment religious strife and upset the secure and unanimous possession of the truth and its religious practice in our country, because while we can allow dissidents to find a means of practicing their religion in Spain, we cannot allow them, against the general will and to the scandal of the people, to proselytize and try to bribe Catholics with gifts away from their religious duties, when virtually the whole nation is determined to preserve its Catholic unity at any price."[14]

This was by no means the end of the propaganda or the difficulties Spain encountered because of Article 6. If anything, they have increased, for Catholic critics have now added their voices

[13] Cf. M. González Ruiz, "El Catolicismo, religión de la Nación," in *Rev. Esp. Der. Canon* 9 (1954), pp. 65-77; E. F. Regatillo, "El Concordato español visto desde fuera," in *Razón y Fe* 687 (1955), pp. 341-60.

[14] Printed in *Rev. Esp. Der. Canon* 8 (1953), p. 839, and in *Ecclesia* (1953-II), pp. 532-3.

to others—critics not satisfied with Cardinal Ottaviani's famous speech delivered at the Pontifical Atheneum of the Lateran on March 2, 1953, *Doveri dello Stato cattolico verso la Religione,* which defended Article 6 as "il caso più tipico" of constitutional recognition. This speech, reprinted in most ecclesiastical and canon law journals, was termed a prologue to the Spanish Concordat. Nor were they satisfied with Pius XII's allocution to Italian canon lawyers, *Ci riesce,* of December 6, 1953, which has been called its epilogue.

The debate continued without any agreement being reached, and Spain continued on her chosen course. Article 2 of the "Fundamental [Constitutional] Law" of May 17, 1958, on the "Principles of the National Movement", stated: "The Spanish nation considers it a point of honor to observe the law of God as defined in the doctrine of the Holy, Catholic, Apostolic Roman Church, the only true Church, and the faith inseparable from the national conscience which will inspire its legislation." (It was in the same "Law" that the political structure of Spain was defined in Article 7 as "traditional, Catholic, social and representative monarchy", which parallels Article 1 of the Constitutional Law of Succession of July 26, 1947: "Spain, as a political unity, is a Catholic, social and representative State which, in accordance with its tradition, declares itself constituted as a kingdom." Because of this and the provisions of Article 9, the head of State must "profess the Catholic religion".[15]

Attempts at Change

Faced with the difficulties of economic, diplomatic, political and confessional pressures, the Spanish State, realizing the hardships its people have been called on to endure, is trying to mitigate the application of Article 6 of the *Fuero*—while respecting its principles—with regard to freedom of publicity for non-Catholic religions, which is the nub of the problem. To this end, Sr. A. Martín Artajo, the Minister of Foreign Affairs (who had also been President of Spanish Catholic Action, and as Minister

[15] Cf. *Leyes Fundamentales* (Madrid, 1964).

had signed the Concordat) sent a letter to the Minister of Justice who, in turn, wrote to the Conference of Archbishops which was meeting in Vitoria. The discussion was extremely serious and of great importance: basic religious principles were at stake and the decision was placed in the hands of the Church, in accordance with Pius XII's ruling in *Ci riesce* (n. 18) ". . . . in the final analysis . . . the Roman pontiff alone is competent [to decide]."

The Spanish Archbishops voted for the maintenance of Article 6, but they had to seek the approval of the Holy See. Rome replied in a letter from Msgr. Tardini, saying that not only should Article 6 be upheld, but that its maintenance constituted a grave duty of conscience, with all the consequences of this.

Later the cardinal primate made a personal visit to Pius XII and set out the same problem, even arguing from the case of Italy which, as a Catholic country of much the same sort as Spain, still allowed greater freedom of activity to non-Catholics. Pius XII's reply was clear: "But we are unable to ask of Italy what Spain can and must give."

The "Statute" and the Council

Then the new Minister of Foreign Affairs, Sr. Castiella (the ambassador to the Holy See when the Concordat was signed in 1953) initiated a whole process of action to obtain a "juridical statute for non-Catholics in Spain". He took advantage of a visit to Pope John XXIII in December, 1961, to gain the Pope's approval to set the process in motion. The statute was drawn up by September 1964, but the Council of Ministers, meeting in La Coruña that month, decided to wait till the Council promulgated its *Declaration on Religious Freedom*.

This and General Franco's end-of-the-year radio and television message (December 30, 1964) had the effect of quieting down foreign pressure until something more definite should be decided. General Franco said: "An important part of the Church's present-day development is the consideration of the most important subject of religious freedom in its true sense and properly understood. Spain faithfully shares this desire that it should be possible in all parts of the world for this freedom to be rightly exercised in accordance with the requirements of the common good. . . . Spaniards should harbor no doubts or distrust on the subject of the exercise of freedom of conscience which we have practiced and which we only desire to perfect in accordance with the authoritative inspiration of our Mother, the Church. . . . Just as Spain has always been in the van of the diffusion of the Gospel, we are not going to find ourselves in the rear of this crusade of brotherhood and love which the Church is now undertaking."

The initiative taken by the Minister of Foreign Affairs has now become the responsibility of the Ministry of Justice, being a matter of legislation for the internal ordering of the country. The Minister of Justice, Sr. Oriol, when he went to Rome during the final session of the Council, on November 13, 1965, for the inauguration of the new Pontifical Spanish College of St. Joseph, discussed this matter in a private audience with Pope Paul VI, emerging well pleased with what had been said.

At the first meeting of the Spanish Episcopal Conference after the Council (February-April, 1966), an Episcopal Commission was set up to establish contact with the Ministry of Justice as a channel of information. The question must remain in the hands of the Ministry because the basic problem of the full application of the Council Decree is fundamentally linked with Article 6 of the *Fuero,* and this Article is incorporated in the two most important and basic juridical documents that it is in the power of any State to draw up: the Concordat for its external relations and its very Constitution (*Fuero*) for its internal ordering.

Therefore, for Article 6 to be changed, not only would there have to be negotiations with the Holy See—inasmuch as it forms part of a Concordat with the Holy See—before it was passed to the *Cortes* (legislative chamber), but also a national referendum on any modification, since it forms part of a *Fuero* (constitutional law). Steps have already been taken in both directions, directly after the Council, with the reservations natural to the case.

The referendum should not prove any obstacle, since Spanish public opinion has been sufficiently prepared by the general tenor of the Council to give up the country's public religious peace for the sake of allowing non-Catholic propaganda in the interests of peace throughout the Church and the world. Furthermore, it will be a law already approved by Rome that is submitted to the people's "referendum" which should finally assuage the conscience of the people. Of course, certain groups, confused by the pressures of the last few years, will adopt a somewhat excessively rigid attitude (cf. the bibliography for and against freedom of religious propaganda—which is the whole nexus of the problem—in the Bibliographical Survey in this volume of *Concilium*), but this is not considered a serious threat. The Spanish people who have borne so many hardships for the sake of the national conscience are not likely to raise any serious objections. On the contrary, their past sacrifices are a guarantee of their fidelity to the new attitudes.

Conclusion

The Spanish people and State are being asked to take up a more ecumenical attitude toward the non-Catholic minority of one in a thousand. With the Episcopal Commission studying the application of the conciliar Decree to Spain in conjunction with the Ministry of Justice, with the Fifth International Congress of Canon Lawyers on the subject of "Law and Religious Freedom" (held in Salamanca, September 8-12, 1965),[16] and with the "John XXIII Ecumenical Circle" functioning in Salamanca under the auspices of the Pontifical University since 1962,[17] the work is already well under way, with the intention of following exactly the lines laid down by the Council. However, the Spanish people have the right to demand in turn that non-Catholics adopt a more ecumenical attitude toward them and cease all abusive propaganda. There are signs that this also is happening, such as

[16] Cf. the article "El Derecho y la libertad religiosa," in *Diálogo Ecuménico* I (1966), pp. 61-9, by José Sánchez Vaquero.
[17] Cf. *Diálogo Ecuménico, op. cit.,* pp. 3-12, 101-2.

the Second National Conference of Evangelical Workers, held in Madrid, October 6-8, 1965, which was attended by some 200 pastors and missionaries from the various Spanish Protestant denominations, and which Catholic observers, not to mention representatives of the foreign press and Dutch television, attended by invitation.[18]

A further clear indication of the new climate is that, during the Christian Unity Octave in January, 1966, the Protestant Juan Alamo Prades was listened to with respect on television throughout Spain. Furthermore, the Monks of Taizé have found the greatest possible understanding and have been accorded all facilities on their visits to Spain, with even the Catholic press giving them wide and favorable coverage.

The problem is one of behavior on both sides. After all, it is logical that the Spanish collective conscience should refuse to tolerate propaganda alien to its faith and should want to conserve and guarantee this right by the formulation of suitable laws.

[18] *Idem,* pp. 75-6.

PART II
BIBLIOGRAPHICAL
SURVEY

Petrus Huizing, S.J./*Heverlee-Louvain, Belgium*

Religious Freedom:
A Bibliographical Survey

W ithin the last twenty years three international organizations have issued Declarations asserting the individual's freedom to determine his own attitude toward the affirmation and service of God as well as his relationship to the various Churches: the United Nations' *Universal Declaration of the Rights of Man* (1948), the World Council of Churches' *Declaration on Religious Freedom* (first issued in Amsterdam in 1948 and again in definitive form in New Delhi in 1961), and the Roman Catholic Church's *Declaration on Religious Freedom* promulgated at Vatican Council II in 1965. All three documents defend the same juridical principle regarding religious freedom: man has an inalienable and personal right to determine his own attitude toward life within the limits of public order without any coercion on the part of civil authority. A great many States have inscribed this freedom into their Constitutions, although it must be added that several States have not yet been able to implement it effectively.

An immense literature has accumulated which deals more or less directly with the problem. In this article I shall mention the principal publications predating Vatican Council II as well as those subsequent to it, including some material that contains further bibliographical data. I thereby hope to present a rather succinct methical survey.

111

1. General and Historical Studies

M. Searle Bates' *Religious Liberty. An Inquiry* (The World Mission of Christianity, VI, New York/London, 1945) remains a basic work in the field due to its wealth of factual and bibliographical information. The book begins with a survey of the actual status of religious freedom throughout the world; it then goes on to pursue the history of religious freedom within the Churches, Christian and non-Christian alike, including a study of the concept, its basis and its place in national and international constitutional law; it concludes with an appraisal and several suggestions in the fields of religion, education, public opinion, politics and law. The author, a professor of history at the University of Nanking, was commissioned to undertake his study by the United Commission for Religious Freedom which was set up by the Federal Council of Christian Churches in the United States in cooperation with five experts from different Protestant denominations. The Italian edition, *La libertà religiosa* (Turin, 1949), was financed by the World Council of Churches.

W. K. Jordan's *The Development of Religious Toleration in England*, 4 Vols. (London: 1932-1940) and Joseph Lecler's *Toleration and the Reformation*, 2 Vols. (New York: Association Press, 1960) deal especially with the history of religious freedom. The latter gives a detailed description of the Protestant and Catholic efforts to bring about religious peace in the 16th and 17th centuries. At that time the matter remained highly theoretical, although many of the arguments brought up then recur in the contemporary discussion of the same theme.

A number of chapters in Jacques Leclercq's *La liberté d'opinion et les catholiques* (*Recontres* 65, Paris, 1963) are devoted to the history of freedom of opinion and, particularly, the development of the Church's teaching regarding it.

2. Freedom of Religion in Political Society

The most complete study of the United Nations' Declaration is probably that of Albert Verdoodt, *Naissance et signification*

de la Déclaration universelle des droits de l'homme (Louvain/
Paris, 1964). It traces remote and proximate origins of the
document, shows in detail how the text came to be framed, com-
ments on each of the articles and contains abundant bibliographical references.

*La liberté religieuse dans les conventions internationales et
dans le droit public général,* by P. Lanarès (Paris, 1964), is
most informative but too one-sided in its interpretation, based as
it is on the liberal theory of Vinet and a distorted presentation
of the Catholic viewpoint.

Mention must also be made of Andrej Bugan, *La comunità
internazionale e la libertà religiosa* (Rome, 1965), H. De Riedmatten, "La liberté religieuse au forum international," in *Etudes*
(1964), and F. Alting von Geusau, "De fundamentele rechten
van de mens," in *Problemen rond de godsdienstvrijheid* (DO-C
dossier, IX, Hilversum/Antwerp, 1965).

Pietro Pavan's *Libertà religiosa e pubblici poteri* (Milan,
1965) contains the text of the articles concerning religious freedom to be found in the Constitutions of the States of Africa,
North and South America, Asia, Australia and Europe; Article
18 of the Universal Declaration of the United Nations; Article
9 of the Convention issued on November 5, 1950, by the members of the European Council on the protection of human rights
and basic freedoms, and the paragraph ratifying the United
Nations' *Universal Declaration* in the Act which established the
Organization of African Unity at the Conference of Addis Ababa
in May, 1963. Finally, the book gives a critical analysis of the
principles underlying these documents and Constitutions. Arcot
Krishnaswami, who reported for the United Nations' subcommission on discrimination and the protection of minorities, published his *Etude des mesures discriminatoires dans le domaine de
la liberté de religion et des pratiques religieuses* (United Nations'
Publication, 60. XIV.2, New York, 1960). I would also refer the
reader to Vroemen's article in this volume of *Concilium.*

3. *The Declaration on Religious Freedom*
   by the World Council of Churches (*New Delhi, 1961*)

Lukas Vischer's article in this volume of *Concilium* describes
the development of the ideas which led to this Declaration.
*Evanston-Nouvelle Delhi, 1954-1961. Rapport du Comité Cen-
tral à la troisième Assemblée du Conseil Oecuménique des Eglises* (Geneva, 1961) gives a survey of what had been done
during those intervening years. The same subject was dealt with
by T. Jiménez-Urresti, "La libertad religiosa ante el proximo
Concilio Vaticano y en el 'Concilio Ecumenista,' " in *Revista
español de Derecho Canónico* 17 (1962).

The Commission of the Churches for International Affairs,
established in 1946, worked hard to draft international norms
and guarantees for the protection of basic human values, particularly freedom of religion. Its representative at the United
Nations was Frederick Nolde, professor at the Lutheran Seminary of Philadelphia. After the United Nations issued its Declaration, the Commission did as much as possible to ensure that
the Declaration was applied in various countries. Among other
things, it followed up the studies undertaken by the United
Nations' subcommission for the prevention of discrimination
(particularly in the religious field) and the protection of minorities; it supported and advised Christian leaders in young countries such as Pakistan, Indonesia, Nigeria, Sudan, Malaysia,
Morocco, Tunisia, Nepal, Madagascar and Somalia, and it provided assistance in countries where religious freedom might be
in danger, such as Colombia, Spain, Italy, Mozambique, the
Near East and some countries of Eastern Europe and Asia. In
1949 a Secretariat for the study of religious freedom was added
to the section for studies; the Secretary for the investigation is a
Spaniard, A. F. Carrillo de Albornoz. The work of the Secretariat is directed by a commission for religious freedom.

Among the publications on Christian principles and religious
freedom, the following must be mentioned: Ernst Gerhard
Rüsch, *Toleranz. Eine theologische Untersuchung und eine ak-*

tuelle Auseinandersetzung (Zurich, 1955; it has an extensive bibliography), E. C. Dewisk, *The Christian Attitude to Other Religions* (Cambridge, 1953) and A. F. Carrillo de Albornoz, *The Basis of Religious Liberty* (London, 1961). *The Ecumenical Review,* 13 (1964), n. 4 (July) contains a symposium on religious liberty.

4. The Declaration on Religious Freedom of Vatican Council II

The most extensive report on how the text was arrived at can be found in T. Jiménez-Urresti's *La libertad religiosa. Declaración del Concilio Ecuménico Vaticano II. Edición bilingue latino-castellana* (Colección de pastoral aplicada, XXIX, Madrid, 1965). The author supplements the text with his own commentary. Points from the debates that took place at the Council obviously will also be found in the reports which appeared during and after the Council.

We might also mention A. Wenger's *Vatican II, chronique de la troisième session* (2 Vols., Paris, 1965), René Laurentin's *Bilan de la troisième session. L'enjeu du concile* (Paris, 1965), and "Das Konzil und das Problem der Religionsfreiheit," in *Herderkorrespondenz* (May, 1964). John Courtney Murray gave a commentary on "The Declaration on Religious Freedom" in Volume 15 of *Concilium.*

T. Jiménez-Urresti was advisor to the Spanish hierarchy at the Council; John Courtney Murray had some influence on the formulation as an expert member of the Commission which drafted the schemas that preceded the Declaration; Pietro Pavan, who had already collaborated on the encyclicals of Pope John XXIII—particularly on *Pacem in terris* with its important passage about religious freedom—was also a member of the Commission as an expert; his criticism of the principles underlying the political documents, mentioned above in section 2, may be considered as an early commentary on the Declaration. See also his article in this volume of *Concilium.*

5. Pre-Conciliar Studies on Religious Freedom

Bevenot, M. "Thesis and Hypothesis," in *Theological Studies* 15 (1954).

Carrillo de Albornoz, A. F. *Roman Catholicism and Religious Liberty* (Geneva, 1959).

Congar, Y.-M "Eglise et état," in *Encyclopédie du Catholicisme*.

D'Apollonia, L. "Tolérance religieuse," in *Relations* 14 (Montreal, 1954).

De la Brière, Y. "A propos de la tolérance civile," in *Miscellanea Vermeersch* (1935).

De Montcheuil, Y. *La conversion du monde* (Brussels, 1944); "Intégralisme et libéralisme," in *L'Eglise et le monde actuel* (1945).

Dondeyne, A. *Faith and the World* (Pittsburgh, 1963); it contains a chapter on "Truth and Freedom" and one on the "Positive Value of Tolerance".

Gross, J. "Religionsfreiheit und katholische Kirche," in *Evangelische Theologie* 9 (1949/50).

Guerrero, E. "Más sobre la libertad religiosa en España," in *Razón y Fe* 149 (1954); "Con la libertad del acto de fe no es incompatible el Estado católico," in *Razón y Fe* 151 (1955).

Jiménez-Urresti, T. *Estado y Iglesia. Laicidad y confesionalidad del Estado y del Derecho* (Victoriensia, Vol. 6, Vitoria, 1958). This is the most basic Spanish study of the theological, philosophical and legal (natural law) aspects of the problem of the denominational State, with extensive references to Catholic and non-Catholic literature.

Journet, C. "Droit de la vraie religion et tolérance civile des cultes," in *Nova et Vetera* 26 (1951), n. 1.

Latreille, A. "Les forces religieuses et la vie politique," in *Le Catholicisme* (Paris, 1951).

Lecler, J. *L'Eglise et la souveraineté de l'Etat* (Paris, 1946); "Les formes modernes de l'intolérance," in *Etudes* 211 (1932); "La papauté moderne et la liberté de conscience," in *Etudes* 249 (1946); "A propos de la distinction de la thèse et de l'hypothèse," in *Recherches de science religieuse* 41 (1953).

Leclercq, J. "Etat chrétien et liberté de l'Eglise," in *La Vie Intellectuelle* 17 (1949); *L'Eglise et la liberté. Semaine des intellectuels catholiques* (Paris, 1952). May be found in *Christianity and Freedom* (N.Y.: Philosophical Library, 1956).

Lener, S. Regular contributions to *Civiltà Cattolica* from 1946.

Lercaro, G. Lecture given at the Dominican theological school of Bologna on April 19, 1958, in *Il diritto ecclesiastico* II (1958); "Religious Tolerance in Catholic Tradition," in *Catholic Mind* 58 (1960), pp. 12-24.

Liberté et verité. A contribution made by the professors of the University of Louvain on the occasion of the bicentenary of Columbia University (Louvain, 1954).

Marcel, G. "Phénoménologie et dialectique de la tolérance," in *Du refus à l'invocation* (Paris, 1940).

Maritain, J. *True Humanism* (New York, 1938); *Rights of Man and Natural Law* (New York, 1943); *Christianity and Democracy* (New York, 1944); *Person and the Common Good* (New York, 1947).

Martinez, G. *Naturaleza juridica e derechos de la Iglesia* (Pamplona, 1954).

Messineo, A. Various articles in *Civiltà Cattolica*, 1950-1952.

Meunier, A. "La Tolérance," in *Revue ecclésiastique de Liège* (1948).

Murray, J. C. "Freedom of Religion: Contemporary Orientations of Catholic Thought on Church and State in the Light of History," in *Theological Studies* 6 (1945); "Current Theology on Religious Freedom," in *Theological Studies* 10 (1949); "The Problem of State Religion," in *Theological Studies* 12 (1951); "Governmental Repression of Heresy," in *Proceedings of the Third Annual Meeting of the Catholic Theological Society of America* (Chicago, 1948).

O'Connell, D. *Christian Liberty* (Westminster, 1952).

Ottaviani, A. Address of March 3, 1953, in *L'Osservatore Romano* (March 4, 1953); *Doveri dello Stato cattolico verso la religione* (Rome, 1953; also published in *Miscelánea Co-millas* 19, 1953); *Institutiones juris publici ecclesiastici*, Vol. I (Rome, 1958-60); *Il baluardo* (Rome, 1961).

Powers, F. *Religious Liberty and the Police Power of the State* (Washington, 1948).

Pribilla, M. "Dogmatische Intoleranz und bürgerliche Toleranz," in *Stimmen der Zeit* 144 (1948/9); "Erziehung zur Toleranz," in *Bildung und Erziehung* 4 (1947).

Rahner, H. *Abendländische Kirchenfreiheit* (Innsbruck, 1943).

Rodrigo, L. "De jure sectandi moralem conscientiam," in *Problemi scelti di teologia contemporanea* (Analecta Gregoriana 68, Rome, 1954).

Rouquette, R. "Pie XII et la tolérance," in *Etudes* 280 (1954).

Salaverri, J. "El derecho público eclesiástico en la Semana de teología," in *Estudios eclesiásticos* 29 (1955).

Semana española de teología (Santiago: Sept. 1954—deals mainly with tolerance and the confessional State).

Tolerance and the Christian (New York: Sheed and Ward, 1955).

Unité chrétienne et tolérance religieuse (Paris, 1950: a symposium).

Verdraagzaamheid (Man and Fellowman) (Utrecht/Antwerp, 1957: a symposium).

Vermeersch, A. *La tolérance* (Louvain, 1912).

Von Kúhnelt-Leddihn, E. "Katholische Toleranz?", in *Wort und Wahrheit* 4 (1949).

Carrillo de Albornoz's study has been called the best synthesis of the Catholic tendency to regard religious freedom as essentially bound up with the Christian spirit of the Gospel. As early as 1959 he could state that the Catholic authors who represent this modern tendency and uphold the general freedom of religion as a "thesis" were so numerous and of such caliber that for every study following the traditional line there appeared ten others in favor of the new one. All of these appeared with the ecclesiastical *nihil obstat,* indicating that the authorities did not think it conflicted with the official teaching of the Church. Of those who clung to the traditional distinction between "thesis" and "hypothesis" he only mentions Martinez, Guerrero, Messineo and Ottaviani, and he points, moreover, to various pronouncements of prominent members of the hierarchy in favor of the modern view. American thinkers show a preference for juridical and political arguments in defense of religious freedom, while the Europeans, with the exception of Maritain, concentrate almost exclusively on biblical and theological arguments. In Albornoz's view, the American approach is based on the conviction that, being one of the "human rights", freedom of religion has no specific problems of its own and can be satisfactorily dealt with juridically, canonically and politically. The European approach also grants that religious freedom is one of the "human rights", but a right with its own special character, since it is immediately based on the absolute relationship between man and God.

6. *Studies that Appeared during the Council*

Alonso, J. *Derechos de la consciencia errónea y otros derechos* (Madrid, 1964); "Diálogo sobre libertad religiosa," in *Verbo,* nn. 37-38 (1965).

Alvarez, J. *El voto de la historia y de la Biblia sobre la libertad religiosa* (Madrid, 1965).

Bea, A. "Libertad religiosa y transformaciones sociales," in *Razón y Fe* 169 (1964).

Bosc, J. "Le respect de Dieu et de l'homme," in *Parole et mission* 27 (1964).

Bronkhorst, A. *See* Dondeyne.

Calvez, J. "Problèmes de la liberté religieuse," in *Revue de l'Action Populaire* (March, 1964).

D'Arcy, E. *Conscience and Its Right to Freedom* (London/New York, 1961); a revised and augmented edition appeared in French, *Plaidoyer pour la liberté de conscience* (Paris, 1964).

De Broglie, G. *Problèmes chrétiens sur la liberté religieuse*

(Paris, 1963); *Le droit naturel à la liberté religieuse* (Paris, 1964); "Essais sur la liberté religieuse," in *Recherches et débats du Centre catholique des intellectuels français,* cahier n. 50 (March, 1965), with the following contributions: G. Aubert, "La liberté religieuse du Syllabus de 1864 à nos jours"; E. Borne, "Le problème majeur du Syllabus: vérité et liberté"; M.-D. Chenu, "Pour une lecture théologique du Syllabus"; R. Remond, "Exigences permanentes de la liberté religieuse"; J. Bergamin, "Le cas d'Espagne: l'Eglise sans la liberté"; N. Struve, "Le cas de l'USSR: l'Eglise privée de la liberté"; M.-D. Chenu, "Exigences présentes de la liberté religieuse"; M.-D. Chenu, with others, "A propos de la liberté religieuse: la modernité de Newman."

Dondeyne, A. and A. Bronkhorst. *Godsdienst—en Gewetensvrijheid* (Patmos series, De Christen in de tijd, 28, Antwerp, 1965).

Freedom and Man. Ed. J. Courtney Murray (New York, 1965) with contributions by: H. Küng, "God's Free Spirit in the Church"; P. Fransen, "Grace and Freedom"; W. F. Lynch, "The Freedom To Be Human"; C. F. Mooney, "Teilhard de Chardin on Freedom and Risk in Evolution"; E. McMullin, "Freedom, Creativity and Scientific Discovery"; R. O. Johan, "Authority and Responsibility"; D. Callahan, "Freedom and the Layman"; J. Y. Calvez, "Possibilities of Freedom in Tomorrow's Complex Society"; C. Malik, "The Metaphysics of Freedom"; K. Rahner, "On the Theology of Freedom."

Gambra, R. *La unidad religiosa y el derrotismo católico* (Seville, 1965).

Garcia Barriuso, P. *Confesionalidad y tolerancia en el Derecho Eclesiástico Español* (Madrid, 1960).

Granero, J. "La libertad religiosa," in *Razón y Fe* 169 (1964).

Guerrero, E. and J. Alonso. *Libertad religiosa en España: principios, hechos, problemas* (Madrid, 1962).

Hernandez, O. "La teología española actual y la libertad religiosa en España," in *Arbor* (Jan. 1964).

Höfer, J. "On Tolerance," in *Gott und Welt,* Festschr. f. K. Rahner (Freiburg i. Br., 1964).

Janssens, L. *Liberté de conscience et liberté religieuse* (Paris, 1964).

Jiménez-Urresti, T. *El ecumenismo en el Concilio y en España. Ecumenismo y libertad religiosa (El Concilio visto por los peritos españoles* (Madrid, 1965, in cooperation with others); "Especial reconoscimiento constitucional a una comunidad religiosa," in *Hechos y Dichos* 360 (Jan. 1966).

Jordan, R. *Libertad de cultos* (Madrid, 1964).

La liberté religieuse. Exigence spirituelle et problème politique (L'Eglise et son temps—Etudes, Paris, 1965) with contributions by: J. C. Murray, "Le problème de la liberté religieuse"; E. Schillebeeckx, "La notion de vérité et la tolérance"; P. A. Liégé, "La liberté religieuse, impératif de la mission" (appeared also in *Parole et mission* 27, 1964); A. Carrillo de Albornoz, "Vers une conception oecuménique de la liberté religieuse"; *Documents du Conseil Oecuménique des Eglises* (New Delhi Assembly).

Le Guillou, M. "Tolérance et liberté religieuse," in *Bulletin du Cercle Saint-Jean-Baptiste* 31 (May 1964); with C. Mercier, *Mission et Pauvreté* (Paris, 1964); "Mission: Obstacle or Stimulus to Ecumenism?", in *Concilium* 4 (1965).

Libertad religiosa. Una solución para todos. Ed. R. Jordan (Madrid, 1964) with contributions by Cantero, De Smedt, Diaz Alegria, Garcia de Enterra, Garcia Martinez, Zalba, Murray, Bea, Boyer, Calvez, Colombo-Lombardi, Perrante, Giacchi, Goffi, Hartmann, Papali, Pribilla, Riedmatten, Rosa, Rugambwa, Vallin, Lercaro.

Liégé, P. "Le droit naturel à la liberté religieuse," in *Parole et mission* 27 (1964).

Lopez Jordan, Rafael. *Libertad de cultos* (Madrid, 1964).

Lumière et Vie 69 (July/October 1964): "La liberté religieuse."

Martelet, G. "La liberté religieuse," in *Rev. de l'Action Populaire* (March, 1964).

Muñoz, J. *Libertad religiosa, aquí, hoy* (Comillas, 1964).

Murray, J. "The Problem of Religious Freedom," in *Theological Studies* 25 (1964).

Nuñez, D. *La libertad de consciencia y de cultos según la razón y la doctrina de la Iglesia* (Buenos Aires, 1965).

Ousset, J. "Variaciones sobre la idea de tolerancia," in *Verbo* 21.

Prieto Rivera, M. *La libre propaganda religiosa en los países católicos* (Seville, 1964; 2nd ed., 1965).

Problemen rond de Godsdienstvrijheid (DO-C, dossier 9) with contributions by: J. Courtney Murray, "De kwestie van de godsdienstvrijheid op het concilie" (with an analysis of the two opposite tendencies at the Council); F. Alting von Geusau, "De fundamentele rechten van de mens"; Report of the World Council of Churches; J. Gonzalez Ruiz, "De godsdienstvrijheid in het nieuwe testament."

Regencia Nacional Carlista de Estella. *Declaración en defensa de la unidad católica de España, frente al Estatuto de seudo-confesiones acatólicas, proyectado por el Régimen* (no date or place).

Rodriguez, V. "Sobre la libertad religiosa," in *Ciencia tomista* 91 (1963).

Schüller, B. "Religionsfreiheit und Toleranz," in *Theologische Akademie* 1 (1965).

Setien, J. "Libertad de consciencia y tolerancia," in *Lumen* 12 (1963).

Unitas (Spanish publ.) 4 (1965), n. 13 (January/April) with contributions by: J. Dalmau, "El diálogo sobre la libertad religiosa"; R. Muñoz Palacios, "La libertad religiosa y sus fundamentos"; P. Suñer, "Consideraciones sobre el derecho a la libertad religiosa"; E. de Enterra, "La libertad religiosa y sus suspuestos límites en los países de unidad católica"; J. Estruch (Prot.), "El protestantismo en España"; E. Colomer, "Libertad y intolerancia en la historia de España"; A. Borras, "La libertad religiosa en el Concilio y en el Syllabus"; J. Aragon Mitjans, "Educacion del niño para la libertad."

Van der Cucht, R. "Autour de la liberté religieuse," in *La revue nouvelle* (May 15, 1965).

Zalba, M. "De iure sequendi conscientiam erroneam in cultu religioso," in *Periodica* 53 (1964); "De iuribus conscientiae invincibiliter erroneae praesertim in re religiosa," in *Gregorianum* 45 (1964).

Note: The Spanish items have been provided by T. Jiménez-Urresti. Some others were pointed out to me by L. Braeckmans, S.J.

7. The Teaching of the Church: Is There Continuity or Is There a Break?

The development of official ecclesiastical doctrine from Gregory XVI to Vatican Council II has been interpreted in different ways. Roger Aubert dealt with the historical and dogmatic background of the papal documents of the 19th century in his contributions to *Tolérance et communauté* (1952) and *Essais* (1965); "Un centenaire. Le Syllabus de décembre 1864," in *La Revue Nouvelle* 40 (1964); "Religious Liberty from *Mirari Vos* to the Syllabus," in *Concilium* Vol. 7 (Sept. 1965); "Le Syllabus," in *Cahiers universitaires catholiques* (Feb. 1965). Gregory XVI, Pius IX and Leo XIII primarily meant to reaffirm religion as something willed by God and therefore to deny a freedom against God. The way in which modern freedom was usually presented and applied at that time endangered these truths, and this is why it was condemned. There is no doubt that Pius IX also aimed at a certain liberal organization of the State, and this constitutes a weakness. The emphasis shifts noticeably when we reach Leo XIII, although he still agreed with Pius IX on many points: the doctrine and certain applications of liberalism remain condemned, but not progress, civil and political freedom and democratic government. Mention is made of a healthy and legitimate freedom, and Aristotelian Thomism recognizes the autonomy of the State in its own field, etc.

Pius XI still condemned "freedom of conscience" over against God and his revelation, but he spoke strongly in defense of "freedom of conscience" with regard to the totalitarian State.

In his Christmas messages during the war, and particularly in his address of December 6, 1953, Pius XII firmly admitted that Catholicism was but a minority in the existing world, and with that the "hypothesis" has become the "thesis", that is, the normal situation, the only one that counts. John XXIII, Paul VI and Vatican Council II confirm what had already become the prevailing teaching of the theologians, namely, that freedom of religion is not a matter of tolerating error and evil but a natural right of man. There is a continuous development from the condemnation of freedom of conscience and neutrality of the State as expressions of rationalism and indifferentism to the recognition of religious freedom with regard to the State's authority on the basis of the respect due to the free personality of man.

Pavan sees this development from Leo XIII to Paul VI as a gradual progress in a straight doctrinal line. Two themes that are constantly recurring are gradually developed. The first is the existence of an objective moral order, unchangeable in essence but with innumerable gradations in the concrete application. This whole order is rooted in the basic relationship between man and God. The life of the individual person, the relations between persons—individually or in some form of community—the relations between citizens and the civil authority and between authorities all over the world are contained within this moral order. The absolute validity of this order is the basis for the obligatory nature of duty and of the inviolability of justice. Authority itself is a requirement of this order and is, therefore, only valid within this order.

The second theme is the central position of the human person in society. This is first established by Leo XIII with regard to the relations implied in man's economic circumstances. Pius XI and Pius XII develop the social and economic content of justice and maintain that the organization of the State should be a service to the human person: general welfare is not an absolute value but is related to the personal good. John XXIII synthesizes the teaching of his predecessors: as a person, every human being is entitled to practice that religion which his conscience demands, even if it does not conform to the objective order—though Pope John recognized that a deepening of the problem was still necessary. His view was already implied in the earlier teaching and brought this teaching to its conclusion. If there is an absolute moral order, and if every human being has the duty to live accordingly, in the measure and manner he understands it, he is *ipso facto* entitled to it as a right, although always within the limits of public order.

John Courtney Murray both criticized and justified Leo XIII's teaching from the point of view of history and sociology. Leo still saw the "prince" as the *pater patriae,* the father of his country, whose "paternal power" had to teach the poor (*miserum vulgus*) and the uneducated (*imperita multitudo*) what was true and good and protect them from error and evil. Sometimes he should be tolerant toward those who were evil-minded in order to avoid worse things in his family. Leo's vision was consistent and was based on the cultural level of his age: hence the paternalistic concept of authority, the confusion of State and society, the ethical concept of the State and the theory of civil tolerance as a hypothesis. Historically this theory is therefore limited to those ideas and not an accurate expression of Catholic teaching. Leo's teaching was not wrong, but it is out of date.

There is no agreement yet about how to interpret the teaching of Pius XII and John XXIII. While Hartmann, Pavan, Courtney Murray and others consider Pius' address of December 6, 1953 a reversal of "thesis" and "hypothesis", Guerrero and Laureano Pérez Mier ("Pio XII y el derecho público," in *Salmanticensis,* 1956) saw it as a confirmation of Leo XIII's views. Some maintain that *Pacem in terris* recognizes everyone's right to serve God according to his conscience, even if erroneous; others hold that this right only belongs to the "right" conscience. One may wish to read more about this question in Victorino Rodriguez, "La 'Pacem in terris' y la libertad religiosa," in *Ciencia tomista* 90 (1963); E. de Regatillo, "La libertad religiosa en Juan XXIII," in *Sal terrae* (1963) and José M. Saiz, "La libertad religiosa

en la 'Pacem in terris,'" in *XXIV Semana española de teología,*
Sept. 1964).

Borne considers that none of the three ways advanced to escape the conclusion that we have broken with the Syllabus is
convincing. Neither the attempt to make the document historically relative, nor the distinction between "thesis" and "hypothesis", nor the interpretation of the document as a prophetic warn-
ing against individualistic freedom in the modern world can
solve the issue which the document presents. It rightly exposes
the evils of a political order divorced from the moral and spiritual order and a conscience detached from all norms, values
or truth. However, it sees no salvation except in a Catholicism
accepted as the State religion because the Roman Church teaches,
with the fullness of truth, a totality of norms and values which
ensure both eternal and temporal salvation. To demand for Catholicism the privileges of a State religion means to forget the
transcendency, the inward character and the universality that are
of the essence of Christianity and to turn it into a form of political absolutism. The Syllabus cannot be rescued from this
philosophically untenable contradiction. It rightly emphasized
certain truths, but at the same time it presupposed such a closed
concept of Catholicism and such an absolutist view that truth
is degraded into a system which is closed to life and freedom.

Chenu (cf. his contribution to *Essais*) sees the development
of ecclesiastical teaching as a process of emergence. Progress usually springs from events—facts that are more or less organic in
character—which become gradually fixed in economic, political
and social structures within which ideologies emerge. *Pacem in
terris* and Paul VI warn against an identification of ideologies
with historical movements, even if the latter spring from the
former. The theologian must then interpret his sources accordingly, without underrating texts of great value in themselves and
without clever apologetics, but rather with the realistic faith
which recognizes that the Christian and human mystery is subject to the law of expression in terms of life on this earth.

Jiménez points out that the conciliar Declaration treats of

freedom from coercion in civil society. It leaves the traditional teaching of the moral claim of revelation and Christ's Church on man and the human community explicitly intact. This theme is also dealt with by J. Leclercq in chapter 8 of *De Pausen en de moderne vrijheden,* "De vrijheid van opinie"; M. Nicolau, "Historia del magistero sobre la libertad religiosa," in *Orbis catholicus* 7 (1964) and his book *Laicado y santitad eclesial, colegialidad y libertad religiosa* (Madrid, 1964).

8. *Freedom of Conscience*

As the basis of religious freedom, freedom of conscience remains a controversial topic. Murray admits that the theory which maintains that the right to religious freedom is founded on the respect due by others and by the State to the honest conscience, even if erroneous, is not to be equated with indifferentism or subjectivism, but he provides no proof; moreover, there is no proof contained in the conciliar Declaration. The question about truth or lack of it in the conscience is not connected with the juridical and social problem of religious freedom. De Broglie rejects this argument just as firmly. Pavan, who seems to admit that the "right" conscience has a natural right to freedom of action, and who also admits that the erroneous conscience has a positive right here for the sake of the general good—i.e., in order to prevent discrimination and to foster the freedom of minorities that have the truth—nevertheless holds that civil freedom of religion lies outside this issue because it is a positive right meant to guarantee a personal right.

A general principle that any action according to a sincere, though erroneous, conscience is beyond the authority of the State is obviously untenable. Therefore, those authors who see in religious freedom a special application of freedom of conscience do not start from the single datum of freedom of action. D'Arcy postulates two Thomistic principles: (1) a man's morality is determined by faithfulness to his own conscience; (2) man does not exist for the sake of the authorities but vice versa. Therefore, he concludes, in contrast to St. Thomas, that natural law forbids the State to compel a man to act against his own conscience. Freedom of religious confession and worship is a particular application of this. Janssens maintains that for freedom of conscience in general, and religious freedom in particular, the decisive elements are the dignity of being subject to morality by which the person himself is responsible for making his free actions be in accord with the judgment of his conscience and his condition as a social being that has to respect the freedom of others. At the same time this indicates the limit of his freedom, since force may be required to see that he maintains this respect.

For Jiménez the central issue of the conciliar Declaration lies precisely in the relation of the objective order, both natural and revealed, to the dignity and reality of the human subject. Among the rights of man, *Pacem in terris* mentioned the freedom to serve God "according to the right norm of his conscience" (*ad rectam conscientiae suae normam*). Does this base the right on the "right norm", in conformity with the objective truth, or on the "right conscience", i.e., the honest judgment of the conscience, even if it judges wrongly? Janssens and Rodriguez have pointed out that the "right norm" is more in the line of St. Thomas, while the "right conscience" is more in the line of Scotus and Suarez. Vatican Council II definitely takes the second line. The norm of the sincere conscience in religious matters is not only valid for private life but also for social life.

9. *The Dignity of the Human Person*

According to John Courtney Murray the objective truth on which the Council based the right to religious freedom is the dignity of the human person. This dignity consists in the ability to act freely according to one's own judgment, out of a sense of duty, without compulsion. The whole social-juridical order rests on this truth, as well as the juridical principle that freedom is the basic norm and coercion can only be justified by necessity. The right *not* to act *against* one's religious conscience is absolute and wholly beyond compulsion; the right to act according to one's religious conscience is limited by public order which may also be maintained by legal force.

In contrast to others, as well as to the State, man has, within the sphere of his own autonomy, the right to act as he wants to, even immorally (De Broglie, Jiménez and others). He even has the right to have this autonomy protected against infringement by the State if necessary. The authors point out that this does not imply the right to immoral action, but only to freedom of action. The sphere of a person's individual autonomy is outside the field of legal compulsion.

10. *Freedom of Faith*

De Broglie does not consider this freedom by itself as a decisive argument for the right to immunity from legal compulsion in the religious field: coercive justice must also be free in its exercise. Jiménez points out that this argument was particularly prominent after the war as a reaction against totalitarian regimes. Professors Vialatoux and Latreille ("Chrétienté et laïcité," in *Esprit*, 1949) maintained that the religious action or the act of faith is the highest form of free action and so excludes any political or legal coercion. Léonard (*Tolérance et communauté*, 1952) added the argument based on the supernatural character of the faith: coercion in this field would imply the presumption to replace grace. But both Jiménez and De Broglie refer to the juridical argument that the inward act of faith falls outside the competence of the law.

Those who, with Janssens, regard religious freedom as a particular application of freedom of conscience nevertheless recognize that it has a character of its own. The religious decision is the most vital one for the orientation of one's life. The supernatural and free character of the faith is the most powerful guarantee for religious freedom. Respect for this is not only a requisite of love and justice, but also of the revealed structure of the faith. According to Chenu this even lies at the very root of the problem of religious freedom. Science yields to evidence which leaves no choice. To believe is to know in and through an intuition of love, an encounter between two persons, a decision which cannot be reduced to its motives, even if these motives are valid, an initiative of God's love which knows of no compulsion, a knowledge born of witness. This knowledge includes freedom. Any pressure, even a social one, devalues not only freedom but also the truth of the faith. Pavan elaborates the social dimension of man's relation to God, the center of the moral order, which is beyond any direct influence from the State and beyond any coercion or pressure from outside. There is no substitute for the light of truth or for the freedom of the spirit. Religious belief cannot be expressed otherwise than in the way it is lived inwardly without losing all religious meaning. The only logical conclusion, then, is that every man has the right to confess his faith as his conscience tells him; it is a right that flows directly from his dignity as a human person; or, as De Broglie and others put it, faith and the expression of faith primarily belong to the sphere in which man is autonomous.

11. *The Argument from Scripture*

For Bronkhorst the argument from scripture is of the first importance. In the parable of the weeds (Mt. 13) the issue is not whether error or even the erroneous conscience has any rights, but about the incompetence of the Lord's servants to separate the wheat from the weeds. This will be done only by the harvesters, the angels, at the last judgment. Neither Peter nor the other apostles are competent to do this. In connection with this we should reflect on the freedom that the father gave to the prodigal son (Lk. 15). Again, in Romans 11, 13, the main purpose of Paul's apostolate among the Gentiles is to stimulate his own people to emulation in order to win over at least some of them; there is not a trace of coercion or oppression of Israel. The New Testament leads to only one conclusion: God does not follow the path of power, coercion, discrimination, spiritual or social terrorism, but that of sacrifice.

G. Ruiz also concludes that scripture imposes respect for the erring conscience (*Problemen*). The "strong" must take into account the conscience of the "weak" (1 Cor. 8, 4-13; 10, 23-33; Rom. 15, 1-15). No one can arrogate to himself the decisive and final judgment. Until then good and evil, truth and error must live in peaceful coexistence (1 Cor. 4, 3-5; 6, 2). For him, too, Matthew 13 is the clearest argument. An analysis of the texts about power and authority shows that the power of the State is not of this world: it even has a demonic tendency. Nowhere is there the slightest suggestion that the State could have a function in the expansion of God's kingdom. The Church submits itself to the State but remains completely independent in its own mission. The use of the power of the State in service of the Church is an infringement of the New Testament concept of religious freedom.

12. *The Incompetence of the State*

That the State is incompetent to exercise coercion in matters of faith and its confession is implied in the autonomy of the person, no matter what arguments are adduced for this autonomy, dignity of the person, the recognition of man as subject to a moral order, freedom of conscience, the nature of the act of faith, the particular nature of man's relation to God, or the scriptures. Some add to this an argument based on the nature of that authority itself. The process of rationalization, applied to the State, has organized this authority in collegiate bodies that decide, by a majority of votes, a way of doing things that is naturally unsuitable when it comes to direct pronouncements about spiritual truths (Pavan). Man's relation to God is not in the service of the State (De Broglie). The political question about the rights and duties of the civil authority, which corresponds to the juridical question about the rights and duties of citizens, finds an answer in the distinction between the two domains of human life, the sacred and religious on the one hand, the profane and the civil on the other. The conciliar Declaration only quotes Matthew 22, 21.

The Middle Ages distinguished between the *sacerdotium* and

the *imperium*. Leo XIII attributed the general temporal welfare to the competence of the State. According to Pius XII and John XXIII, even this is limited by the higher order of the rights of man, among which the right to religious freedom occupies a special place (Courtney Murray). Jiménez sees the social ordering of religion as a hypothetical function of the State in natural law—i.e., if this function had not been given to the Church through a positive institution by Christ. The present factual incompetence of the State in these matters is a theological reality.

13. *Competence of the State and the Limits of Religious Freedom*

Various authors have indicated various criteria by which to determine where freedom of religion ceases to have a claim to immunity from coercion by the State, and where the State's right to compel therefore begins. According to De Broglie, the first limit is the rights of other people, not only as individuals but also on the social level of general welfare; this latter element goes well beyond the mere protection of particular individual interests. Legal coercion can prevent infringement of other people's rights, and also all that is noticeably harmful from the social point of view. Certain ways of antisocial conduct can be stopped, as can activities that go against the basic requirements of social life, or which disturb the psychical balance, like spiritualist seances. Opposition to specific actions or even whole religions is only possible when they themselves run counter to the basic requirements of elementary social morality. D'Arcy mentions the fact that the Australian High Court refused exemption from military service for reason of religious objection because it held that to impose something on somebody that has nothing to do with religion is not the same as to prevent him from freely exercising his religion. The author concludes that the law and the judge cannot decide what is true or not true in religion, but he can decide whether a particular point of faith is correctly presented as exercise of religion; otherwise every action could be exempted from the authority of the State simply by labeling it as religious.

In the theories put forward by John Courtney Murray and Janssens, this criterion is superfluous. The former says that the theory according to which the authority has the moral and legal duty to prevent religious error and evil has been rejected by Pius XII and the Council. The author also rejects the theory which bases the right to repression on general welfare, since the care for this general welfare is not exclusively the task of the authority, while religious freedom is a part of that welfare. The Council accepted the theory that it is not welfare at large, but one element of it—namely, a public order that implies elementary justice, a minimum of morality and real peace and offers the sound criterion of public behavior, even when inspired by religious motives—that can be prevented legally as an infringement of the law when it violates the rights of others, affects public morality or endangers public peace.

Janssens objects to Article 29, §2 of the *Universal Declaration of the Rights of Man:* "In the exercise of his rights and the enjoyment of his liberties, every man is only bound by the limits fixed by law with the exclusive aim of ensuring that the rights and liberties of others are recognized and respected and of complying with the legitimate demands of morality, public order and general welfare in a democratic society." This formula does not explicitly exclude the authority from deciding the contents of morality, public order, general welfare and democracy. More personalistic in approach are the words, "limits fixed [by] . . . the demands of general welfare", if we understand this general welfare as the conditions for living together, working together and sharing together in the fruits of this togetherness. This idea excludes measures that would conflict with human dignity, since such measures could never be required by general welfare, the basic condition of which is precisely human dignity. It is the function of the State and all international organizations to make each man respect the dignity of all: hence the need for limitations that are based only on temporal general welfare and not on one or another religious conviction and therefore are equally applicable to all, whatever their philosophy of life.

Jiménez sums up the teaching of the Council as follows: The natural limitations of the natural right to religious freedom form the basis for a just public order, namely, the protection of civil rights which imply religious freedom and the peaceful ordering of this freedom, social peace, the maintenance of public morality and the equality of all citizens before the law, without discrimination. The declaration of the Spanish bishops at the close of the Council on December 8, 1965, rightly states that these limitations on religious freedom may differ according to the different social structures of various countries.

In connection with all this, Schillebeeckx has pointed out that there is no sense in stretching the principles of tolerance so far that they imply tolerance of intolerance in principle or in fact. The State, too, has to take measures against the propaganda of organizations that attack freedom of conscience. In border cases tolerance may have to use coercion.

14. *Religion and the State*

If the State is not competent to deal with religious matters, this does not imply indifference. The lack of competence concerns value judgments about the contents of religion; it does not mean that the State cannot put at the disposal of the citizens such means as may help them to cultivate and assimilate these contents. In this case the State has a positive function similar to its function with regard to science, the arts, etc. (Pavan).

It is not the function of the State to promote religion itself but rather the free social exercise of it, since this is a human right and an element of the general welfare with a corresponding duty on the part of authority. The Council does not deny that the State has a moral function and a duty to assist the citizens' moral and Christian life by means of just laws and good government. This obviously is part of the temporal order.

Apart from the maintenance of public order, the State has

many functions with regard to the general welfare (Murray). It is the duty of the State to see to it that everyone enjoys the objective living conditions which allow him to live according to his personal convictions. Freedom of religion and one's philosophy of life is a positive value: hence the function of the State to promote the development and education of the various groups, at least proportionately and according to distributive justice (Schillebeeckx).

Even the most neutral State cannot be wholly indifferent toward all religious groups; even if it is indifferent about specific aspects, such as the religious teaching about God and man, the State, whether neutral or confessional, will encourage these groups insofar as they have a good influence on social morality (De Broglie).

The State must support religious communities, not because of their philosophy of life, but solely on a sociological basis (Janssens).

Apart from maintaining public order, even by coercion, the State has a wide field of care for the general welfare which implies no compulsion, and to this field belong religious values insofar as they are part of the social order. This is not a religious matter but a temporal one. It flows from the State's functional subordination to the value of religion, as to that of the arts, science, economics, etc. It is not a religious duty (*religio*) toward God in a direct sense, but a duty of justice toward the citizens (Jiménez).

15. What About the Confessional State?

A modern expression of the "thesis" was formulated by De Broglie, who holds that the simple and basic concept of the State is not the neutral one but the confessional one. Neutrality is motivated by accidental reasons that demand a compromise and can take all kinds of shapes without unconditionally supporting or rejecting any of them. Religious truth can never be part of the compulsory public order, but the general welfare *does* include spiritual and moral values, for which both citizens and the State are responsible. These values imply as large a share of religious and moral truth as possible and also the fidelity to this truth. Catholic citizens and officials need not behave as if they were atheists or agnostics. The only kind of State that can fulfill its function completely is the Christian State which not only promotes the fundamental principles of social morality but also the true religion. Instead of being only interested in the "ideal" of the neutral State, Catholics ought to be able to affirm the value of the Christian State while remaining aware of the fact that this concept includes all the openness and goodwill demanded by ecumenical love with regard to other religions. For the rest, the personal commitment of those in authority is more decisive than the particular form a State may have.

Pavan admits that there may be situations where it is opportune or necessary for a political community to assume a religious qualification and to state in its Constitution that legislation and government must be inspired by principles taken from a specific historical religion. But even then the religious freedom of every citizen must be assured and no one must be placed in a position of civic inferiority for reasons of religion. This could easily lead to political pressure, and this, in turn, to a contortion of the religious life.

According to John Courtney Murray the conciliar Declaration wants to avoid the impression that the concept of a paternalistic Catholic State which excludes other religions from its public life has any theological foundation. The explanation and justification in such a case would be wholly due to historical circumstances. If a religion is given any legal privileges, this must not exclude the freedom of others. The Declaration does not go beyond this. It does not deal with the uneducated masses, still always a reality in traditionally Catholic regions. Can the State still claim a "paternal power" there? This is a question of fact, and facts yield no conclusions about principles. It is moreover an exceptional fact that cannot provide a basis for juridical standards.

Dondeyne maintains that there is no universally valid solution possible for regulating the legal relations between Church and

State. The main point is to find a formula that guarantees both the sound running of the State and the free movement of the Church. To discover this formula and a way of putting it into practice is primarily the task of the Christian politician.

Chenu speaks of the Christian State as a failure, or worse, an error. The knowledge of faith is so personal that it cannot be treated as a thing that one possesses. This insight cannot be materialized in institutions that turn it into a collective possession and then impose it simply because of the fact that one belongs to this collectivity. When the Church, the community of the faithful, and thus faith itself get fixed in an impersonal way of setting about things, as they do when they let themselves be caught in temporal structures, however legitimate in themselves, then indeed Christianity has discovered its limits. To treat heresy as a crime against the State is the same kind of conduct as erecting unbelief into a law of the State.

Liégé admits the logic of the abstract arguments in favor of a Christian State—arguments that hold for any "established" Church—but he has simply no faith in them from the missionary and evangelical point of view. He asks how in such a case one can distinguish what is God's from what is Caesar's, between error and erring people, between truth and those who accept this truth in conscience. He inquires how one can recognize the transcendence of the Church, the inner nature of faith, the patience of Christ's proclamation, the poverty of the Church's powers and the hope of a Christlike victory. A neutral State that protects religious freedom is preferable to that. The Catholic Church demands no privileges on the ground of truth, but only respect for the religion the citizens confess in various ways.

According to Jiménez the principles that are valid for the religious freedom of the individual are, by analogy, applicable to the community. The conciliar Declaration provides the immediate motive for a special legal recognition of one or more specific religions, a recognition that applies to Spain, England or Sweden as well as to Islamic, Jewish or Buddhist States: the special situation of a people or the collective conscience of a people. Just as the individual knows God's law through his conscience, so it is with the community. Its juridical order does not immediately envisage the objective order, but it looks at this objective order through the medium of the collective conscience. The principle of religious freedom also holds for the political community, so that one is not compelled to act against the collective conscience or prevented from acting according to this conscience. That, too, is a natural right, and this freedom also has to respect the rights of others, whether persons, groups or other countries, and it must take into account the general welfare on an international level. Finally, international political organizations must act as the Sub-commission of the United Nations already does and watch States where abuses take place under pretext of religious freedom.

16. *The Principle of Reciprocity*

Pribilla has published the text of a letter written in 1233 by Gregory IX to the French bishops. The pope writes that Christians must treat Jews with the same kindness they themselves would expect in pagan countries. Hartmann considers this a basic argument. The appeal to truth cannot be meant to be effective in a community of nations where this truth is only recognized by a minority. There the only valid principle is that of a justice which is intelligible and acceptable for all. D'Arcy considers this a missionary motive. If the Church wants to win over those who are alien to it, it must show the world a face that the world can recognize as the face of Christ. Christians can only be recognized as Christ's disciples if they love non-Catholic minorities like themselves and therefore treat them as the Christians themselves would want to be treated if they were in a minority. Jiménez also sees the conciliar Declaration in this light. Religious freedom is one of the signs of our age. The growing international and pluralistic unity of mankind makes it increasingly impossible for one specific faith or religion to determine the membership of a political community and the enjoyment of civil rights. On the other hand, what is taken most seriously today and what is most respected in mutual relationships is precisely what corresponds to religious conviction and conscience as the highest and most intimately human value. Although the proclamation of Christ and his Church remains universally valid, the immediate norm for religious conduct is each one's own honest conscience. The conciliar text means a genuine progress in the positive appreciation and respect for the human conscience in national and international law.

This bibliographical survey is limited to the juridical and political aspects of religious freedom, such as it is presented in the conciliar Declaration. The most recent publications among those already mentioned look toward further questions: the consequences of this freedom for ecumenical cooperation between the Christian Churches, the relations with non-Christian religions, the dialogue with atheism and the problem of the Christian missions. Several authors, such as Borne and Schillebeeckx, are already pointing to a deeper ground for the right to religious freedom, namely, the personal respect for another's conviction as such, as the way in which each at one time or other shares in the truth. Above all, a religious freedom, which is not merely juridical but is valid throughout the length and breadth of society, confronts the Church and individual Catholics with the question about the freedom with which they really live their own belief in Christ, and about a training in this freedom. The right to religious freedom will only protect those from withdrawal into their own ghetto or loss of their own conviction who can live their own faith and convictions in inward personal freedom. It will then enable them to create a true community with people and groups who have other convictions.

Ivan Žužek, S. J./*Rome, Italy*

Notes on Religious Freedom in the Christian East

No more than notes are given here, and there are two reasons for this. First, a bibliographical survey would not permit more. Second, the subject is totally new, it seems, and would require a detailed study to give a really balanced idea on what religious freedom meant and means in the Christian East. However, one hopes that these notes present a relatively good survey on the matter, and, further, that they may open a path for research in a new and tempting field.[1]

I

EASTERN FATHERS AT THE COUNCIL

The conciliar interventions of the Eastern bishops on religious freedom were few and of no special significance as regards the doctrine of Vatican Council II on this subject. However, they

[1] In this bibliographical survey the pages quoted in the text in brackets refer to the works in the bibliography at the end of the article. The bibliography is divided under the same headings as the article itself. It is a very pleasant duty to express here my most sincere thanks to Very Rev. Archimandrite J. Cotsonis (Athens), Rev. Prof. M. Wojnar, O.S.B.M. (Washington, D.C.), Prof. H. Alivisatos (Athens), Prof. M. Belić (Zagreb) and Prof. S. Trojanos (Athens) for valuable indications on the literature for this article.

are noteworthy for having shown the unusual unanimity of the Eastern fathers in supporting the *Declaration on Religious Freedom*. Eastern Catholic Churches are minority communities in the midst of an atheistic, Moslem or acatholic world. Religious intolerance, hatred and often persecution have been their daily bread throughout history. Their very existence is a miracle, proscribed as they are in some countries by inexorable law, but the miracle continues underground. It is understandable why it was an Eastern bishop, Most Rev. M. Doumith, who addressed the Council, in the name of 70 fathers from the Middle East, Africa and Asia, to suppress the last clause of section 5 of the schema (*textus reemendatus*) of the Declaration, which propounded the ideal of the *status confessionalis*. The terms would have been misunderstood by Moslems for whom religious law is the source of the civil law, which leads to discrimination between the "faithful" enjoying all rights in the State and the "unfaithful" suffering constantly a *deminutio capitis*. Against the same text Bishop I. Ziadé also spoke, and doubtless for the same reasons. In rejecting the special right of a religious community to regulate the State by its laws, he said that: (1) this contradicts the whole document; (2) it explicitly approves religious discrimination; (3) it is injurious to the Gospel, since Christians should obey any legitimate authority and should not ask in return any special protection from the State; and (4) it is regulated by the principle *cuius regio, eius religio*. The interventions of His Beatitude, Patriarch Paul Meouchi, and of Cardinal J. Slipyj, Ukrainian Major Archbishop, were favorable to the Declaration, but their forceful arguments had a more general character not reflecting the special position of Eastern Catholic minorities.

II

The Freedom of Religion in Orthodox Authors

To Prof. H. Alivisatos, the well-known Greek canonist, I am deeply indebted for a kind letter with a few guidelines toward the understanding of the Orthodox view on religious freedom. He mentioned a few works and attributed the lack of a wider literature to the truly democratic nature of the Orthodox Church wherein freedom of belief is rarely discussed, for it is one of the most substantial elements of St. Paul's teaching and, therefore, a necessary characteristic of the Church.

There were Russian canonists at the beginning of this century who produced some good works on religious freedom. The occasion was the State law of April 17, 1905, enacting freedom of belief for the Russian Empire. The best authors, like Berdnikov, Sokolov, Krasnožen and some others, gave substantially the same teaching as the majority of pre-conciliar Catholic authors. A summary of such opinions is to be found in Krasnožen's *Cerkovnoe pravo* (*Canon Law*, pp. 303ff.) of 1917:

1. All force in the spreading of Christian faith is prohibited; the only weapon that the Church has in this field is the Word.

2. The Church, convinced that membership in it is necessary for salvation, cannot be indifferent to the spreading of its faith and to the prohibition of "proselytism" or religious propaganda of all other doctrines.

3. It may not attempt to extend by forcible means its laws and rites to the members of other Churches.

4. Neither, on the contrary, may it be forced to grant its sacraments to those who are not its members.

At the turn of the century there were still many clerics in Russia who openly considered forcible means as honest when employed against the enemies of the Church. However, the best Russian thinkers felt that this was in contradiction to genuine Orthodoxy.

Tolstoi rebelled, calling the Church which used such means a "worldly and unchristian institution".

Chomjakov's (d. 1860) chief idea on Orthodoxy was that it is the synthesis of unity and liberty in charity. He accused Catholicism of sacrificing liberty in favor of unity, and Protestantism of having done the contrary.

Dostoievski's world-famous chapter on the "Great Inquisitor" in *The Brothers Karamazov* was, perhaps, the real turning point for many minds. Its real meaning was that the crucified Truth cannot use force in drawing all men to himself. Dostoievski blamed the Spanish Inquisition, but still more he blamed, in this chapter, every "theocratic state" (the Russian Empire among the first), as of its nature bound to deny liberty of spirit and conscience.

Dostoievski and Chomjakov were the masters of Berdiaev's (d. 1948) theology, which was founded on the concept of God as the abyss of liberty, and which at times led the author to a real insubordination to any directive from the Church.

Bulgakov (d. 1944) was a friend of Berdiaev. He too openly professed that sins against liberty inevitably are sins against Orthodoxy, the Church and the Holy Spirit. When Bulgakov's teaching on "Sophia" was officially condemned by Orthodox hierarchies, Berdiaev saw in this the "spirit of the great inquisitor" and openly protested that there was much more liberty in the Catholic Church than in Orthodoxy (*Put'*, n. 49, p. 75), though formerly he had asserted just the opposite (*Die Ostkirche,* p. 5).

Religious freedom is not the same as insubordination to Church authority, but from the above it seems certain that Vatican Council II's *Declaraion on Religious Freedom* will be welcomed by the Orthodox world as the clearest formulation of a truth common to East and West. The Right Reverend Emilianos Timiadis, in a talk given in Rome in November, 1965, accepted the Declaration as an ecumenical need.[2]

Little can be drawn from the canons of the Eastern Churches in regard to religious freedom. All they stress is freedom in accepting Christian baptism and the prohibition of all force in the propagation of the faith. The Archimandrite, Jerome I. Cotsonis, in a brief but fine article of 1963, enumerated the respective canons and concluded that the Church in its legislation

---

[2] I express here my sincere thanks for the manuscript. It will be published before long under the title "La libertá religiosa come esigenza ecumenica."

never permitted the use of coercion in the propagation of the faith, but, on the contrary, it always tried to secure the free choice of those who accepted the Christian faith. He admits that there were cases in the history of the Eastern Church where the propagation of the Gospel took place through coercion, but they were deviations from the right way, indicated by the Lord, canon law and the Fathers of the Church like Gregory of Nazianzus and Athanasius the Great. These deviations could not change the rule. Canon law itself, though obligatory and at times enforceable by ecclesiastical penalties, "has as an absolutely necessary prerequisite the free entry into the Church" (p. 111).

III

PROSELYTISM AND RELIGIOUS FREEDOM

For Orthodox authors, the most acute question touching religious freedom and the ecumenical movement is that concerning proselytism. The Ecumenical Patriarchate issued in January, 1920, an encyclical letter to all Christian Churches in which the eradication of proselytism between the Churches was proclaimed as a necessary preliminary condition to ecumenical contacts. The representatives of the Greek Church, guided by Prof. H. Alivisatos, made the same request at the World Conference on Faith and Order in Lausanne in 1920, in view of a common effort of all Churches in missionary work in non-Christian lands.

Milaš (p. 467) stated in 1926 that the Orthodox Church (meaning all of them) peremptorily prohibits every kind of proselytism among Christian nations. The claim of the Orthodox, however, seemed to be somewhat contrary to religious freedom. According to the New Delhi Assembly of the World Council of the Churches, this included also the "freedom to teach, whether by formal or informal instruction, as well as preaching with a view to propagating one's faith and persuading others to accept it".

The Orthodox produced a series of writings to explain their point of view, the best of which was that of the Right Rev. Chrysostomos Konstantinidis, representing the Ecumenical Patriarchate, and a few pages in *Orthodoxia* of 1961 written by an anonymous author. In this last article the distinction of ecumenists between Christian witness (μαρτυρία) and proselytism is fully accepted, though it is hard to see where one ends and the other begins. According to Zander (p. 258) the distinction between Christian witness and proselytism is very subtle. It refers rather to the intention of the will than to the content of the preaching. While proselytism always maneuvers to destroy the spiritual structure already formed in others, thus intruding upon their consciences, witnessing avoids violence and moral pressure and leaves the initiative of an eventual "conversion" to others. Zander's view here is hardly acceptable, since a positive law cannot permit witnessing and prohibit proselytism if there is only a difference of intention between them. Zander finds no theoretical grounds for abstention from proselytizing by honest means, but upholds it as a necessary postulate of ecumenical reality, which otherwise becomes a revolting struggle between Christians who seek to convert each other. Of course, this presupposes that baptized heretics and schismatics can be saved by other paths than by a formal adherence to the true Church. "If this were not so," says the same author (p. 263), "abstention from proselytizing would be either a crime or a sign of indifference not only to the truth but to my erring brother."

Proselytism may be understood in different ways:

1. Christian witness, that is, public profession of one's faith without any intention to convert others. Even so, it is prohibited or much restricted in the U.S.S.R. and some other countries.

2. Religious propaganda by honest means with the intention to convert: (a) non-Christians (in this case it is called missionary work), or (b) Christians taken individually. Religious propaganda taken in this sense is called proselytism by the Greek Orthodox. It is rejected as preventing sincere ecumenical relations. In fact, this is a weighty reason, since ecumenism has to

be taken seriously, but it seems to be the sole argument for this position. The principles of religious freedom would admit such proselytism. It was categorically prohibited for the non-Orthodox in czarist Russia.

3. Religious propaganda by dishonest means: such proselytism falls, of course, under the prohibition of the natural law. One has a strong impression that the majority of ecumenists regard proselytism exclusively as this sort of propaganda. Carrillo de Albornoz (p. 401) takes the word to mean the "perversion of religious witness by the use of the wrong unevangelical means". In the same sense it is understood in the Message and Resolutions from the Middle East Christian Youth Leaders' Consultation of 1955: "The Churches should always avoid seeking to win members of the other Churches by offering special advantages, economic or otherwise, by moral pressure, by taking advantage of difficult situations in another Church or by misrepresenting its tenets." Greek State law also prohibits only so-called "criminal proselytism". Law 1363/1938, in Art. 4, reads as follows: "Proselytism is an immediate or mediate endeavor by presents of any kind, or by the promise of such or other moral or material aid, by deceptive means, by the abuse of skill or confidence or by the exploitation of need, of spiritual weakness or simplicity, with a view to the penetration into the religious conscience of those of another religion, for the purpose of changing its content. That this practice is performed in a school or formative or philanthropic institution is considered as a particularly aggravating circumstance."

The same article declares that such actions are punishable by imprisonment and a monetary penalty of 1,000 to 50,000 drachmas, and further by police supervision, the duration of which, from 6 months to 1 year, is determined by a judicial sentence. The Greek Code protects the Established Orthodox Church from proselytism in a particular manner. The canonists treat of these laws in the manuals of canon law, but the laws seem at times to go too far. A father who tries to divert his son (over 14 years of age) from the Established Orthodox Church commits the crime of proselytism. This, for instance, goes beyond the limits of religious freedom.

Paragraph 4 of the *Declaration on Religious Freedom* of Vatican Council II settles the matter in a truly ecumenical spirit. It affirms the right of Christian witness, but repels all dishonest means in the spreading of the faith:

"Religious bodies also have the right not to be hindered in their public teaching and witness to the faith, whether by the spoken or by the written word. However, in spreading religious faith and in introducing religious practices, everyone ought at all times to refrain from any manner of action which might seem to carry a hint of coercion or of a kind of persuasion that would be dishonorable or unworthy, especially when dealing with poor or uneducated people. Such a manner of action would have to be considered an abuse of one's own right and a violation of the rights of others." [3]

It is noteworthy that this text speaks of Communities, not of individuals. Whatever apostolic zeal an individual person may feel, he should know that it belongs to the authorities of the Church, which he believes to be the true Church; he must limit his thirst for the conversion of others whenever this would lead to actions contrary to the natural dignity of the human person, to the unsettling of good faith in the members of another Church or to an injury to ecumenism.

IV

RELATIONS BETWEEN CHURCH AND STATE

For a long time the Byzantine world was governed by the theory according to which the State was strictly obliged to

[3] *"Communitates religiosae ius etiam habent, ne impediantur in sua fide ore et scripto publice docenda atque testanda. In fide autem religiosa disseminanda et in usibus inducendis abstinendum semper est ab omni actionis genere, quod coercitionem vel suasionem inhonestam aut minus rectam sapere videatur, praesertim quando de rudioribus vel de egenis agitur. Talis modus agendi ut abusus iuris proprii et laesio iuris aliorum considerari debet."*

eradicate as far as possible every error or sin, as being against the common welfare. This theory is now rejected by many Orthodox authors and it is considered erroneous by Vatican Council II, as explained by J. C. Murray in a recent article. Until the conquest of Constantinople by the Turks on May 29, 1453, it is almost impossible to distinguish between canon law and the civil law; therefore, a short outline of the relations between Church and State in the Christian East seems indispensable for an understanding of the questions connected with religious freedom.

1. *In the Byzantine Empire*

Leaving aside theological considerations, the difference between the teaching of Catholic and Orthodox canonists may be briefly expressed as follows. The Catholic position concerning the relations between Church and State was summed up in the formula of Pope Innocent III (*P.L.*, 214, 377): the Church is the sun; the State is the moon. For Orthodox, until recent times, the idea rather was that, as far as the law (not dogma) is concerned, the State is the sun and the Church the moon. It is also true that in the East some churchmen, such as the Russian Patriarch Nikon, used the term "sun" for the patriarch and the term "moon" for the czar. Orthodox authors, like Panagiotakos, call the Catholic teaching of the supremacy of the Church over the State *theocracy* or *hierocracy*. They have in mind more the teaching of the Bull *Unam Sanctam* of 1302 on the direct power of the pope over the State (which was abandoned long ago) than more moderate theories of Catholic authors. *Caesaropapism* for the Orthodox means only an order of things in which the Church becomes merely a government body for ecclesiastical affairs (e.g., Henry VIII in England, Peter I in Russia). In the so-called *politeiocracy* (πολιτειοκρατία) all real juridical power is in the hand of the monarch who, however, recognizes the Church as a special spiritual power and therefore gives it all the necessary support. If to this is also joined the concept of the monarch as *epistimonarches*—that is, the guardian of the Church—it is easy to understand why he often claims some special rights in strictly ecclesiastical affairs.

It was not easy for Christian emperors of the late Roman Empire to understand that the Gospel stripped them of the office of *Pontifex Maximus*. A code of laws of March 31, 726, *The Ecloga,* even stated in its preface that God bade the emperor, as he bade St. Peter, to feed his most faithful flock. *The Ecloga* was included in some canonical collections (e.g., in the Russian *Nomocanon* of 1653). Such ideas were still strengthened in the 12th century by two outstanding canonists, Theodorus Balsamon and Demetrius Chomatenus, as is well explained in a recent article of Troicki. They said that the emperor, because of his anointing at his coronation, was endowed with special ecclesiastical rights which made him a sort of *episcopus episcoporum*. Both canonists recognized in the emperor even the right of nominating bishops and patriarchs and freedom from the ecclesiastical canons. However, these and similar ideas were rather the exception than the rule, though they strongly influenced some canonical literature, such as the *Syntagma of Matthew Blastares*. In the *Nomocanons* (Codes of Canon Law) the so-called theory of harmony was propounded, by which a perfect harmony should reign between Church and State, since both powers flow from the same source. This theory was most clearly formulated in the sixth *Novella* of Justinian, and it was then incorporated into almost all *Nomocanons*. However, the theory of harmony never succeeded in drawing a neat line between the competence of the two powers. Not the Church, but the emperor, usually by himself, decided how far he would go in his quality of guardian of the Church. This was the Achilles tendon of this very evangelical and, to a great extent, ideal theory. It was only natural that the theory in practice led in most cases to a real *Caesaropapism,* to an almost complete subjection of the Church to the State. The head of the State was in practice, and at times in theory, also the head of the Church. As far as the subject's religious freedom, he had to be intolerant of anything which could endanger the religious unity of the State. In actual fact the territorial principle *cuius regio, eius religio* governed the Byzantine world long before it was expressed in the West.

The laws concerning religious intolerance found in Byzantine legislation were numerous. For the first century after Constantine the Great they are briefly outlined (e.g., in Greenslade). The *Codex Theodosii,* especially in *Liber XVI,* is full of measures restricting, or better abolishing, religious freedom. The same is true for the *Codex Justiniani* and for the whole subsequent Byzantine legislation.

2. Constantinople under the Turks

The Byzantine *politeiocratic* ideal came to an end in 1453. Muhammed II, the conqueror of the city, astutely secured the consolidation of his empire by instituting a new patriarch and giving him political and religious jurisdiction over the "whole nation of Christians". The Turks, at least in their official attitude to the Greek Church, observed the principles of the *Koran* that "there is no compulsion in religion" (II, 258) and that "the people of the Gospel judge by that which is revealed therein" (V, 51). The Church seemed more free than ever, but basically it was still subordinated to the Sultan. He changed patriarchs so often that the average duration in their office for these centuries was no more than two years. "The Christian nation" as distinct from "the faithful" was submitted to many discriminatory restrictions of religious and civil rights, and thus many of its members were tempted to abandon their faith under morally compulsory measures. In spite of some official declarations proclaiming civil equality of Christians and Musulmans, in some Moslem States even today the Christians are still considered only as second-class citizens.

3. Modern Greek Church

With the proclamation of Greece as an independent kingdom in 1832, the Greek Church proclaimed itself autocephalous.

However, its freedom from the State was completely lost. The king became the head of the Church, with the right to exercise the veto against any decree of the Synod of Bishops. In 1923, in a new Charter, Cavour's principle was applied to a "free Church in a free State", but in 1932 it was changed again so as to arrive at a system much more similar to the ancient theory of harmony. This system is called by Panagiotakos "the system of government in force by law". The Church is free in what regards the *sacra interna,* but everything that regards *sacra externa*— that is, whatever touches the external order of the community— has to be sanctioned as State law and carried out by the civil power. The Established Church, says Panagiotakos (*Ekklesia,* p. 286), is recognized as "an absolute and spiritual power, with its own form of government and its own sphere, operating and acting in order that in the State, sooner or later, the reinforcement of the laws and political good may be obtained". Other religious communities may be recognized as "known religions", and as such they enjoy legal protection in their public cult under two conditions: (1) their internal regulations should not be contrary to the State law, and (2) they should abstain from "prohibited proselytism".

The least free in Greece seems to be the Greek Church itself. The recent revolt against the law of 36 Greek bishops, in the election of candidates for vacant sees, created scandal among the Greek people, but it has perhaps turned upside-down the legal foundation of the Church in Greece. The Right Reverend Archimandrite Jerome I. Cotsonis did not hesitate in a recent talk to declare himself in favor of a complete but gradual separation between Church and State (under certain conditions), as it is related in *Service Oecuménique de Presse* of January 6, 1966.

4. Bulgarian and Rumanian Churches

Before World War II, in Bulgaria there reigned a similar system to that in Greece. The Bulgarian Constitution of 1947, however, enacted complete separation between Church and State and denied any privileged status to the Orthodox Church. A special law on religious denominations of February 17, 1949, allowed, in Art. 3, the Orthodox Church to be "the Church of the Bulgarian People's Republic" because "it is the traditional religion of the Bulgarian people", strictly "linked with its history". Other religious denominations are also free to perform their religious obligations if they do not violate the laws of the State, do not disturb public order or good customs and are not exploited in favor of political propaganda. The statutes of every Church have to be approved by the government. The education of young people and children is reserved exclusively to the State.

The Statutes of the Rumanian Orthodox Church were approved by the Presidium of the General Assembly of the State on February 23, 1949. This Church is considered as a public institution. The Patriarch Justinian, questioned in 1955 on the possibilities of coexistence between the Church and a government guided by a materialist philosophy, replied: "The aim of the Church and of the Popular Democracy is one and the same: man. Church and Popular Democracy are both pursuing the happiness of man; they both pursue social justice and an equal distribution of material goods. Thus there exist many points of agreement between Church and State. Certainly there also exist some points of controversy . . . but what is the good of enumerating them?" (cf. *Orthodoxy,* p. 230).

The Ecumenical Review of 1961 published some "Notes on Religious Liberty in Eastern Europe" (pp. 497-501) which seem to be the best judgment on the matter. The "Notes" warn that in these countries the administrative pressure on the Churches varies greatly from time to time and from country to country, that "the liberty of religious confession" in the sense of personal faith and "worship" is less than "religious freedom" as defined in the Universal Declaration of Human Rights, and that this liberty, exercised "according to the law", is in fact easily curtailed or violated by the law, which is apparently considered to be above the rights of the human person.

5. Russian Orthodox Church

The Byzantine system of harmony between the two powers dominated the Russian stage until the middle of the 17th century. Church and State were, on the whole, tolerant toward religions of the newly conquered nations, but there was no pity toward Orthodox who turned heretics. The Russian Inquisition followed Spanish patterns. Recently Bolshakoff published a fine book which fully justifies this assertion. Some heretics were executed even before Novgorod's Archbishop Gennadius (1484-1504) became an "admirer of the Spanish Inquisition, the methods of which he had learned from Nicholas Poppel, the Western emperor's ambassador" (p. 33). Joseph of Volokolamsk exposed Gennadius' views in his *Prosvetitel* (Enlightener). He demanded at a synod of Russian bishops in 1505, against the followers of Nilus of Sora, that heretics should be excommunicated and delivered to the civil authorities to be burned alive. Nilus taught that the human conscience is free and that no one should be persecuted for his religious beliefs. At the synod, however, the severe point of view prevailed, and it remained substantially unchanged until modern times, though in the 19th century other punishments for heresy were imposed in place of burning. Even as late as 1739 three monks of the sect of Chlysty were executed, and, to complete the matter, the two bodies of the founders of the sect (who died respectively in 1700 and 1716) were disinterred and solemnly burned. The Chlysty were a group of madmen rather than a very dangerous sect. Peter the Great (1682-1725) was more tolerant. The Russian Old-Believers could worship God their own way, provided they paid a special tax, wore special garb and abstained from religious propaganda of any kind. True, the laws against heretics were at times inoperative, but in some periods, as under Nicholas I (1825-1855), they were applied with severity.

At the end of the 19th century Uvarov's formula of "Orthodoxy-Autocracy-Nationalism" governed the State and the Church. The members of other beliefs were considered as potential traitors. Throughout the history of Slavic nations such formulas produced the worst effects of religious intolerance. Because being Orthodox meant to be a Russian (or Serbian) and being Catholic meant to be a Pole (or Croat), religious intolerance between Orthodox and Catholics was directly proportioned to the hatred that obtained between Russians and Poles, Serbs and Croats. The consequences were disastrous and are best described in Gogol's *Taras Bul'ba*. This hatred is the very contradiction of Christian love and the penalty for it is today's struggle for existence of the Churches in all Slavic countries.

Krasnožen, in *Inovercy na Rusi* (Heterodox in Russia), in 1903 distinguished freedom of conscience from: (1) freedom of the hierarchical organization of a Church; (2) freedom in public worship; and (3) freedom to form associations on religious grounds. He said that any Christian State must recognize the full freedom of conscience, but it should not allow the other three freedoms to be unlimited because this would be to the detriment of the truth represented by the State. Therefore, the legislation should not only grant some special favor to the Established Orthodox Church, but by every legitimate means protect, defend and spread its faith. As a consequence the Russian laws gave full rights to the Orthodox Church to proselytize anyone within the limits of the Russian Empire; however, under grave penalties such as exile or jail, it prohibited any heterodox religious propaganda directed toward diverting Orthodox from the Established Church.

About April 17, 1905, when many restrictions of religious liberty were abolished—although the Established Church remained in a favorable position—there were many pamphlets and essays on this subject in Russia. What was said ranged from the most conservative point of view to the most liberal opinion of a total separation between Church and State. A proclamation of 32 parish priests of St. Petersburg declared that the "liberation of the religious conscience from external restraint is welcomed with great spiritual joy by all true members of the Orthodox Church. The Church will at last be cleared of the heavy charge of violating and suppressing religious freedom. This was formerly done in its name under the pretense of defending it, but it was done against its will and against its spirit" (cf. Zernov, p. 67).

The least free of all Churches in Russia, however, remained the Orthodox Church. The movement to free it from the "protection" of the State was crowned with success only after the fall of the czar, "the Protector", in 1917. At the national synod of that year words such as the following were heard (related by Kartašev, p. 48): "We have had enough of the union with the State; our bones cracked in the iron embraces of the protector-State. We do not need carriages and distinguished positions; we shall walk on foot and be free, as the sectarians are [from 1905 on], and be supported by our faithful people." Nevertheless, the Church passed a lengthy resolution requesting from the State, already Communist, some privileges for the Orthodox Church. It based its demand on no theological grounds, but on the mere fact of its being the Church of the majority. The Communists answered this request by the law of January 23, 1918, which, though proclaiming freedom of conscience, stripped the Church of every right, stating in article 12 that no religious society may be entitled to own private property or have the rights of a juridical person.

V

UKRAINIAN AND RUMANIAN CATHOLIC CHURCHES
OF THE EASTERN RITE

In modern times there is no Church in the world which has endured as many sufferings and continual persecutions as the Ukrainian Catholic Church, under the czars, at times under Latin Catholics and, finally, under the Communists. The czars in 1839 and 1875 forcibly annexed all Uniate Ukrainian parish churches in Russian territories to the Established Orthodox Church. When in 1905 religious freedom was to some extent recognized and many of these forced Orthodox proclaimed themselves Catholics, the Orthodox authors had to admit that such "apostates" had never been Orthodox, that "they did not enter the Church of their own will, but were driven into it by Cossacks' whips" and that in 1905 "they did only what any prisoner does when the door of the jail is left open" (cf. *Cerkovnyj Vestnik*, 1906, col. 1269). One prefers quoting Orthodox opinions in order to avoid any prejudice. The action of the czars was imitated by the Bolsheviks in 1946 when, by threats, imprisonments and concentration camps, about 5,000,000 Ukrainian Catholics were forced again to "reunite" with the local Orthodox Church. The story is inhuman to the utmost, and it was repeated in Rumania in 1948, in Užhorod in 1949 and in Slovakia in 1950. Why the local Orthodox Churches uttered not a single word of protest is quite a legitimate question, but one that is extremely embarassing for the age of ecumenical movement. Perhaps one may hope for a restoration of the Ukrainian Catholic Eastern Church.

The Appeal of November 12, 1965, signed by all Ukrainian bishops abroad (except Cardinal J. Slipyj, for obvious reasons) and presented to the Council, was eminently justified. The Appeal invited all the Council fathers: (1) to promote prayers in every diocese in the world for the restoration of the Ukrainian Catholic Church in the U.S.S.R.; (2) to invite civil authorities to take the initiative (by Soviet Union Representatives of the United Nations) for the same end. A detailed *Memorandum* was joined to the Appeal, describing the sufferings of Ukrainian Catholics.

One could also express here the hope of the restoration of the destroyed Rumanian Catholic Church of the Eastern Rite, and this in the light of the "freedom of conscience and belief" proclaimed in the same Rumanian Constitution. This flourishing Church, numbering more than a million and a half Catholics, was declared inexistent by a governmental decree of December 1, 1948. The facts leading to this were the following: (1) on July 17, 1948 the Concordat with the Holy See of 1927 was unilaterally abrogated; (2) on August 4, the General Decree on Religious Denominations was issued in which Art. 37 stated that if 75% of the members of any given Church adopt another one, all goods of the former become the property of the new one; (3) on October 1, a "synod of 36 Uniate priests" (no bishop was present) was gathered together by the police in Cluj and it "revoked" the Union with Rome, signed 250 years earlier in Alba Julia.

BIBLIOGRAPHY

I

EASTERN FATHERS AT THE COUNCIL

For the intervention of Patriarch Paul Meouchi, cf. *Antiochena* 7 (1965), pp. 9-10; also cf. pp. 13-14 for the intervention of Bishop Ziadé and p. 15 for the intervention of Bishop Doumith. The summary of the intervention of Cardinal Slipyj is in *L'Osservatore Romano*, September 17, 1965.

II

THE FREEDOM OF RELIGION IN ORTHODOX AUTHORS

Berdnikov, I. *Naši novy zakonoproekty o svobode sovesti*, Moscow, 1914 (Our New Schemes of Laws on Religious Freedom).

Sokolov, A. *K godovščine veroterpimosti v Rossii*, Astrachan', 1906 (On the Anniversary of Religious Tolerance in Russia).

Krasnožen, M. *O veroterpimosti i ee granicach*, Jur'ev, 1905 (On Religious Tolerance and Its Limits).

For the opinions of Russian authors on this subject, cf. Simeon (Hieromonk), *Russkaja literatura po voprosu o svobode sovesti i pravil'naja postanovka etogo voprosa*, Kazan', 1905 (Russian Literature on Freedom of Conscience and the Right Determination of This Question); M. Krasnožen, *Ukazatel' literatury cerkovnogo prava*, Jur'ev, 1910 (Index of Canonical Literature), Appendix to the *Zapiski Jur'evskogo Universiteta* n. 9, under Arseniev, Bobrovskij, Kantorovič, Kiparisov, Kuznecov, Poznyšev, Poljanskij, Prugavin, Sapožnikov, Sil'vester, Titov, Cvetaev and Špakov; cf. also *Cerkovnoe pravo* (Canon Law) of the same author, published in Jur'ev in 1917, for the continuation of the Index on pp. 185-89.

Tolstoj, L. N. *O veroterpimosti*, St. Petersburg, 1906, an extract from *Vsemirnyj vestnik* (On Religious Tolerance).

Chomjakov, C. *L'Eglise latine et le protestantisme au point de vue de l'Eglise d'Orient* (Lausanne, 1872), pp. 59ff., 64ff.

Berdjaev, N. *Mirosozercanie Dostojevskogo*, Prague, 1923 (Conception of the World of Dostoievski); *O naznačenii čeloveka,* Paris, 1931 (On the Destiny of Man); *O rabstve i svobode čeloveka,* Paris, 1933 (On the Slavery and the Freedom of Man); "Duch Velikogo Inkvizitora" (The Spirit of the Great Inquisitor) in *Put'* 49 (1935), pp. 72-82; "Orthodoxie und Ökumenizität," in *Die Ostkirche, Sonderheft der Vierteljahresschrift "Una Sancta"* (Stuttgart, 1927), pp. 1-16.

Bulgakov, S. posthumus edition of *Avtobiografičeskie zametki,* Paris, 1946, cf. p. 44. (Autobiographical Notes)

The opinions of other Russian thinkers may be found in two books of B. Schultze, under the word "Freiheit" in the General Index: *Die Schau der Kirche bei Nikolai Berdiajew, Orientalia Christiana Analecta* 116 (Rome, 1938), and *Russische Denker, ihre Stellung zu Christus, Kirche und Papstum* (Vienna, 1950).

Cotsonis, J. "Freedom and Coercion in the Propagation of the Faith," in *The Greek Orthodox Theological Review* 9 (1963), pp. 97-111.

III

PROSELYTISM AND RELIGIOUS FREEDOM

For the encyclical letter of 1920 and the proposals of H. Alivisatos in Lausanne, cf. *Istina* 2 (1955), pp. 93-99, and G. I. Konidaris, "The Position of the Catholic Orthodox Church in the League of Churches," in Θεολογία 20 (1949), pp. 301-13, 495-523 (*in Greek*).

Milaš, N. *Pravoslavno crkveno pravo,* Beograd, 1926 (Orthodox Canon Law).

For the text on religious freedom of the New Delhi Assembly, cf. *The Ecumenical Review* 16 (1964), p. 401, n. 1; 14 (1962), pp. 457-58.

Konstantinidis, Chr. "Proselytism, the Ecumenical Movement and the Church," in Θεολογία 28 (1957), pp. 517-31; 29 (1958), pp. 18-36, 169-82, 497-511; 30 (1959), pp. 153-78 (*in Greek*).

Orthodoxia 36 (1961), pp. 32-44, "Christian Witness, Proselytism and Religious Liberty in the Concept of the World Council of Churches" (*in Greek*).

Zander, L. "Ecumenism and Proselytism," in *The Ecumenical Review* 3 (1951), pp. 258-66.

Carrillo de Albornoz, A. F. "Religious Liberty and the Second Vatican Council," in *The Ecumenical Review* 16 (1964), pp. 395-405.

For the Message of the Middle East Christian Youth Leaders, cf. *The Ecumenical Review* 7 (1955), p. 395.

Christofilopoulos, A. P. "The Reception into the Orthodoxy of Unbaptized and Heterodox," in Θεολογία 27 (1956), pp. 53-60, 196-205 (*in Greek*).

For the Greek legislation, cf.:

Fillipidou, T. G. "Crimes against Religion in the Greek Penal Code," in Θεολογία 26 (1955), pp. 223-58; on proselytism, cf. pp. 247-58 (*in Greek*).
Panagiotakos, Pan. I. *The System of Canon Law in Force in Greece*, Vol. III, Athens, 1962; on proselytism, cf. pp. 383-404 (*in Greek*).
Mourike, G. "Constitutional Protection of Religious Liberty," in *Archeion ekklesiastikou kai kanonikou dikaiou* 11 (1956), pp. 34-42, 133-38, 221-28; 12 (1957), pp. 32-38, 90-96, 161-66; 13 (1958), pp. 43-48, 171-78; 14 (1959), pp. 29-34 (*in Greek*).

IV

RELATIONS BETWEEN CHURCH AND STATE

Murray, J. C. "La Déclaration sur la liberté religieuse," in *Nouvelle Revue Théologique* 98 (1966), pp. 41-67.

1. *In the Byzantine Empire*
Panagiotakos, Pan I. *Church and State during the Centuries: 33-1939*, Athens, 1939 (*in Greek*).
Troicki, S. "Crkveno-politička ideologija Svetosavske Krmčije i Vlastareve Syntagme," in *Glas Srpske Akademije Nauka* CCXII, Section for Social Sciences, Beograd, 1953, pp. 155-206 ("Ecclesiastico-Political Ideology of the Nomocanon of St. Sava and of the Syntagma of Matthew Blastares").
Greenslade, S. L. *Church and State from Constantine to Theodosius*, London, 1954.
Alivisatos, H. "Les deux régimes dans l'Eglise unie avant la schisme," in *Etudes L. Beauduin* 2 (1955), pp. 105-16.
Reilly, G. *Imperium and Sacerdotium according to St. Basil the Great*, Washington, 1945.
Stefanidou, B. "The Final Position of the Evolution of the Relations between the Church and the Byzantine State and Its Immediate Consequences," in *Epeteris Hetaireias Byzantinon Spoudon* 23 (1953), pp. 27-40 (*in Greek*).
Dvornik, F. "Byzantine Political Ideas in Kievan Russia," in *Dumbarton Oaks Papers* IX-X, Cambridge, Massachusetts, 1956, pp. 73-121.
Zankov, S. *Četiri glavi v/rchu problemata za otnošenieto meždu C/rkva i D/ržava*, Vol. 22, 1945 (Four Chapters on the Problem of the Relations between Church and State).

2. *Constantinople under the Turks*
Papadopoulos, Chrys. "The Position of the Church in the Turkish State after the Fall of Constantinople," in Θεολογία 12 (1934), pp. 5-24, 97-115 (*in Greek*); "From the History of the Church of Constantinople during the 19th Century," in Θεολογία 21 (1950), pp. 3-18, 141-58 (*in Greek*).
Papadopoulos, Th. M. *Studies and Documents Relating to the History of*

the Greek Church and People under Turkish Domination, Brussels, 1958.

Fattal, A. *Le Statut légal des non-musulmans en pays d'Islam,* Beirut, 1958.

De Vries, W. "La Chiesa nella Turchia moderna," in *La Civiltà Cattolica* 93 (1942), n. 2203, pp. 16-21; n. 2204, pp. 92-97.

Douglas, E. H. "The Theological Position of Islam concerning Religious Liberty," in *The Ecumenical Review* 13 (1961), pp. 450-62.

3. *Modern Greek Church*

A bibliography until 1957 may be found in S. Nanakos, "Staat und Kirche in der griechischen Orthodoxie," in *Ostkirchliche Studien* 6 (1957), pp. 268-81. Also worthy of mention are:

Panagiotakos, P. I. "General Observations on the Position of the Religion and the Church in Greece according to the Actual Constitution," in *Archeion ekklesiastikou kai kanonikou dikaiou* 7 (1952), pp. 3-24 (*in Greek*); "Considerations on the Impending Crisis between State and Church in Greece," *ibid.,* 20 (1965), pp. 49-79 (*in Greek*).

Georgiou (Metrop.), "Relations between Church and State," in *Archeion ekklesiastikou kai kanonikou dikaiou* 6 (1951), pp. 155-71 (*in Greek*).

Poulitsas, P. "Die Beziehungen zwischen Staat und Kirche in Griechenland," in *Die orthodoxe Kirche in griechischer Sicht,* Vol. II, Stuttgart, 1960, pp. 33-48.

4. *Bulgarian and Rumanian Churches*

Zankov, S. *Die Verfassung der Bulgarischen Orthodoxen Kirche,* Zürich, 1918).

Kirill (Actual Patriarch), *Katoličeskata propaganda sred B/lgarite prez vtorata polovina na XIX vek,* Sofia, 1962 (Catholic Propaganda among Bulgarians in the Second Half of the 19th Century).

Deset godina na B/lgarskata Patriaršia, Sofia, 1963 (Ten Years of the Bulgarian Patriarchate).

Cavalli, F. "Persecuzione religiosa nella Repubblica Popolare Bulgara," in *La Civiltà Cattolica* 104 (1953), n. 2462, pp. 138-52.

La Documentation Catholique (1949), cols. 1205-09, "Les lois sur les cultes en Bulgarie."

Orthodoxy 1964, Athens, 1964.

Georgescu, P. *Beiträge zum Verhältnis zwischen Staat und Kirche in Rumänien,* Bucharest, 1913.

Mateiu, I. *Politica bisericească a Statului românese, Sibiu,* 1931 (Ecclesiastical Politics in the Rumanian State).

A good bibliography on the Rumanian Church is in *Lexikon für Theologie und Kirche,* Vol. 8, 1964, pp. 98-99.

5. *Russian Orthodox Church*

Bolshakoff, S. *Russian Nonconformity,* Philadelphia, 1950.

Zernov, N. *The Russian Religious Renaissance in the Twentieth Century,* London, 1963.

Kartašev, A. *Cerkov' i gosudarstvo*, Paris, 1932 (Church and State).
Krasnožen, M. *Inovercy na Rusi*, Vol. I, Jur'ev, 1903 (Heterodox in Russia).
Medlin, W. K. *Moscow and East Rome. A Political Study of the Relations of Church and State in Muscovite Russia*, Geneva, 1952.
Troickij, P. S. *Otnošenie gosudarstva k Cerkvi po vozzrenijam najbolee vidnych našich pisatelej i obščestvennych dejatelej*, Moscow, 1909 (The Relations between State and Church in the Views of Our Most Distinguished Writers and Social Workers).
Struve, N. *Les chrétiens en U.S.S.R.*, Paris, 1963.
Teodorovič, N. A. "Processi e condanne contro i sacerdoti e credenti nell'USSR 1956-1965," in *Russia Cristiana* 7 (1965), pp. 13-25.

V

UKRAINIAN AND RUMANIAN CATHOLIC CHURCHES
OF THE EASTERN RITE

Memorandum sulla persecuzione della Chiesa Cattolica in Ucraina, Rome, 1965.
Gadžega, J. *Stat'ji po voprosam pravoslavija, narodnosti i katoličestva*, Užhorod, 1911 (Articles about the Questions of Orthodoxy, Nationality and Catholicism).
Lužnickij, A. *Ukrains'ka Cerkva miž Schodom i Zachodom*, Philadelphia, 1954 (The Ukrainian Church between East and West).
Korolevskij, C. *Metropolite Andre Szeptyckyj, 1865-1944*, Rome, 1964.
Primi incatenati (libro bianco sulla persecuzione in Ucraina), Rome, 1953.

For Užhorod and Slovakia, cf:

Lacko, M. "The Forced Liquidation of the Union of Užhorod," in *Slovak Studies* 1 (1961), pp. 145-85.
De Vries, W. "Soppressione della Chiesa Greco-Cattolica nella Subcarpazia," in *La Civiltà Cattolica* 101, Vol. II (1950), pp. 391-99 (German trans. in *Stimmen der Zeit* 146 (1950), pp. 70-72).

For the Rumanian Catholic Church, cf.

Tocanel, P. *Storia della Chiesa Cattolica in Romania*, Padova, 1960.
De Vries, W. "Religionsverfolgung in Rumänien," in *Stimmen der Zeit* 146 (1950), pp. 120-26.
Biserica Română Unită (various authors), Madrid, 1952 (United Rumanian Church).
Gsovskij, V. *Church and State behind the Iron Curtain: Czechoslovakia, Hungary, Poland, Romania, with an Introduction on the Soviet Union*, New York, 1955.

For other authors, cf. *Lexikon für Theologie und Kirche*, Vol. 8 (1964), pp. 98-99 (bibliography by E. Herman and O. Bârlea).

The best study on the Soviet Union is *The Church and State under Communism. A Special Study Prepared by the Law Library of Congress for the Subcommittee to Investigate the Administration of the Internal Security Act and Other Internal Security Laws of the Committee on the Judiciary and the United States Senate*, Vol. I: parts I, II, III, *The U.S.S.R.* (Washington, 1964-1965 (for the Ukrainian Catholic Church, cf. part III, pp. 66-71).

PART III
DO-C DOCUMENTATION
CONCILIUM

Office of the Executive Secretary
Nijmegen, Netherlands

Petrus Huizing, S.J./*Heverlee-Louvain, Belgium*

Should the Church's Marriage Laws Be Revised?

Vatican Council II has been the subject of widespread publicity. It would be difficult to underestimate the role of this publicity in determining the course of the Council and the results it achieved. In the meantime, a revision of canon law is in progress. To a very large extent the outcome of this revision is going to determine the actual effect of the Council on the life of the Church. Therefore, I feel it is extremely important that this revision be exposed to public opinion both from within the Church and the world at large.

In this article I would like to contribute my opinions to the discussion on how the ecclesiastical order concerning marriage should be revised. This will bring to the fore some rather fundamental issues. The technical and juridical resolution of these issues is the task of canon lawyers, but the problems themselves demand a less one-sided study.

1. *The Contents of the Consent Given in Marriage*

The *Pastoral Constitution on the Church in the Modern World* states: "The intimate marital communion of life and love, instituted by the creator and ordered by his laws, comes about through the marital agreement, i.e., through an irrevocable personal consent." This consent is the "human deed by which the partners give themselves to each other and accept each other"

(n. 48). The question is whether the Council intended to promulgate a new notion of the essential content of marriage and, therefore, of the marital consent different from that defined in canon 1081, par. 2: "The consent to marriage is the free action by which a man and a woman give each other and accept from each other, for always and exclusively, the right to each other's body for the performance of actions that by their nature are aimed at procreation." Does this new formulation put the principal emphasis on the community of life and love and no longer on a claim to marital intercourse as in the old juridical view? The question is a basic one for all of marriage law. Whether the ecclesiastical community recognizes a marriage as valid or not depends primarily on what this community regards as the essential content of marriage and, therefore, of the marital consent involved.

It seems to me that the contrast between a community of love and a juridical community, so current nowadays, is really based on a misunderstanding, particularly a misunderstanding of this point. Marriage is defined by the fact that man and wife bind themselves to each other precisely in view of their sexual difference, and this for life. In doing so they present each other with the possible issue of their bodily union, or, in other words, they mutually bestow the claim to parenthood. This definitive mutual gift is an expression of love which can best be rendered in terms of justice. Paul already did so in the most concrete manner: the husband's body is no longer his but his wife's, and the wife's body is no longer hers but now belongs to her husband. The bond of justice does not rule out the bond of love; on the contrary, it shows the force of this bond of love. In this case, law is the love which makes itself the norm and reason for the irrevocability of the bond and deprives itself of the possibility to take back what has once been given. In this, marriage refers to the bond which obtains between Christ and his Church, a bond which became an irrevocable right in Christ's incarnation.

2. The Completeness of the Consent Given in Marriage

The conciliar Declaration reemphasizes the "irrevocable personal consent" as the sole cause of a marriage. As such it must embrace the entire essence of marriage. Its irrevocable character and binding force is not imposed by law from without, for the two partners themselves want it this way. If this is not their intent, then they are not yet married and, therefore, not irrevocably bound by it. This logically inescapable consequence creates a whole series of questions for canonical teaching and jurisprudence:

(a) Is it correct to maintain that, on the basis of canons 1086, par. 2 and 1092, par. 20, the *positive* exclusion of one essential element of marriage can be reason enough for nullity? Is not a marriage prevented just as much by the *negative* lack of an essential element in the consent given? Moreover, can this negative lack not be established with moral certainty? For instance, can a teenage marriage which disintegrates within a few months reasonably be considered as an alliance originally intended for life, even if the participants had been dreaming of a lifelong partnership?

(b) Canon 1082 requires as a minimum understanding of marriage that the parties know that marriage is a lasting bond between man and wife which by its very nature is intended for the purpose of founding a family. Can one always consider this knowledge as sufficient without checking whether the consent given "virtually" implied the full realization of what marriage entails? Of course this is possible. The actual consent can, and usually and naturally will, imply more than conscious knowledge. But is this necessarily so? For instance, a girl that has had even minimal instruction about bodily sexuality will normally surrender herself to her husband in such a way that she accepts the real implications of this spontaneously and actually gives her consent. But if in an extraordinary case the realities have not been accepted, can one still maintain that this acceptance was nevertheless willed "implicitly" or "virtually"?

(c) According to canons 1083 and 1084 the simple misunderstanding of certain essential elements of marriage or of the other party's circumstances does not invalidate consent. Within the context of current teaching and legal practice this means that consent is only invalidated by a positive objection to some essential element of marriage or by making some quality, which the other party does not possess, a condition for consent. Is this right? Suppose a young man marries a girl because she has led him to believe that she is pregnant by him. After the wedding it is discovered that she was actually pregnant by someone else, and the young man leaves her at once. When he gave his consent he did not think that deception might be involved, and so he simply said "yes" without any such proviso as "on condition that I really am the father of your child". Does this mean that he accepted the girl unconditionally? Insofar as the content of his consent was concerned, nothing "essential" was lacking, but the very existence of his consent was "existentially" and totally due to a situation created by deliberate deceit. Can one maintain that his consent is still binding within the context of the real situation?

Usually, though not necessarily, this question crops up in situations where serious deception is involved. In such cases extreme pressure is applied from many sides demanding that a positive declaration be introduced which would make the consent obtained by such deception null and void. The question may be asked whether this is not a norm of natural law (possibly to be put under the category of "implicit conditions").

(d) Canon 1068 makes *physical* impotence—the permanent inability to engage in conjugal relations—an impediment to marriage based on natural law. But would the *moral* impossibility of undertaking a permanent and exclusive mutual relationship *a fortiori* invalidate a true marriage? The Roman Rota has accepted this in the case of nymphomania, a psychological deviation which compels a woman to promiscuity in such a way that she lacks moral responsibility for her behavior. She is, therefore, incapable of binding herself exclusively to one man, even if she wanted to. It is obvious that the same norm must also be equally valid for the man. If we are to be consistent with this principle and follow it to its logical conclusion, we will have to apply it much more broadly. For example, if the man to whom the woman gives her consent happens to be a sadistic psychopath, is this tragic discovery merely a matter of a "simple misunderstanding on some circumstances or quality"? Is it not rather corroboration of the fact that he is incapable of contracting a genuine marriage? When it is clear almost from the start that the mutual bond rests upon a complete misapprehension, and when it can be established objectively that a lasting communion of life and love between two people is clearly a moral impossibility, is it not obvious that they wanted to achieve something of which they were manifestly incapable, namely, a genuine marriage?

(e) Canon 1087 says that consent inspired by fear of serious threats or unjust duress is null and void. But cannot the high degree of human freedom demanded for this consent be affected by inner psychical compulsion? Take the case of a girl living at home under the truly oppressive tyranny of her parents. Although she tells herself she is in love with a young man and marries him, she is in fact merely unconsciously driven by the desire to escape from her oppressive family atmosphere. Was her consent a personal and free action? One can hardly call personal surrender that which is in fact an escape from an intolerable situation.

In all these questions it is not a matter of introducing new principles into the canonical order of marriage. It concerns the consistent application of a truth that is wholly traditional, namely, that the sole foundation of a marriage is the act of personal marital consent. The objection can be raised, and in fact has already been raised, that this approach extends the possibilities for nullification still further and in doing so further undermines the social stability of marriage. That is possible. Nevertheless, the legitimate development which has taken place since Pius XII, and most emphatically in *Pacem in terris* and various conciliar documents, will also make itself felt in Church law and particularly in laws pertaining to marriage. In the past the paternal or—less pleasantly expressed—the paternalistic coercion of family, society and authority could in many ways supplement personal freedom without attacking it. Today the situation is changing. The keynote of all efforts to achieve societal order is becoming more and more the respect for the personal dignity and freedom of man. It is no longer acceptable to maintain that, because of the social stability of marriage, one can impose a binding marital relationship on people who cannot or will not undertake such an imposition. The Church order now has to take into consideration each one's personal situation as it exists in fact. The stability of Christian marriage must now be borne by the personal conviction of the Christians. The Church can help them with this through preaching and pastoral care, but no longer through presumptive juridical situations that are not valid existentially.

3. The Presumption of Validity

This leads us naturally to the principle contained in canon 1014, namely, that the legal presumption is in favor of marriage. Its most important application is contained in the norm that, in case of doubt about a marriage, this marriage is presumed to be valid unless the contrary is proved. One of the classical arguments is the statement of Innocent III; "One should rather tolerate that some remain united in marriage against the laws of man than that some who are lawfully united should be separated against the laws of God" (X 2. 20, c. 47, *Licet ex quadam*). The interpretation of this text is far from simple. Several of the older canonists found it just as questionable to declare a marriage relationship lawful when genuine marital dispositions were lacking as to declare a lawful marriage unlawful. The main argument adduced in defense of canon 1014 is that when there is a conflict between public and private interests, the former prevail. In case of doubt regarding the validity of a marriage, separation may be in the interest of the partners but certainly not in the interest of the children and the social stability of marriage. But is it not of equal social importance not to impose marriage on people who are not husband and wife and have no intention to be? In case of doubt this is just as much of a risk.

Perhaps we can escape this dilemma by a consistent application of what has been said above concerning a reappraisal of the free personal decision. If someone wants his marriage nullified merely because of a purely formal juridical defect—for instance, the unauthorized delegation of the priest who assisted at the marriage—then there is every reason for requiring definite proof. The decision to dissolve a marital bond which involved genuine intent on such formal grounds as these can only be morally justified when such a defect is definitely established. But the case is different when there is genuine doubt about the integrity of the marital consent. In such a case the personal decision to consider oneself free of a commitment that is objectively doubtful can find moral justification. (This should obviously take place without prejudice to the obligations which one certainly has toward the other partner or the children.) It appears that it is not, or at least is no longer, the duty of the law to exclude this decision *a priori*, but rather to respect it as long as it is not certain that it lacks moral justification. How often does it happen that someone wants to legalize before the Church a second marital situation which evidently rests on a genuine disposition for marriage, while it is not certain, but rather truly doubtful, whether his previous marriage was genuine? It can even be so doubtful that at different stages in the proceedings different judges have handed down opposite decisions. In this uncertainty the Church can help people to decide in a personal and responsible manner rather than decide for them.

Pius XII warned the Roman Rota repeatedly against a too rigorous application of canon 1014 (in his addresses of Sept. 3, 1941 and Oct. 1, 1942, and more strictly still in the Codex commission of June 26, 1947). This proves at least that problems are involved which must be subject to a fresh reexamination.

4. The Competence of Church and State

The two partners who bind themselves in marriage necessarily claim by the same token that others recognize and respect their marital contract. A marriage is inevitably a community affair. One cannot claim communal recognition for any random agreement. The community can, through those entitled to speak in its name, refuse to recognize a marital bond that does not satisfy the legitimate conditions, such as a public ceremony, or one that transgresses generally accepted norms, such as a marriage between blood-relations. A marriage that is not recognized by the legitimate community on reasonable grounds is no marriage.

Which community is decisive for recognition? Canon 1016 states: "The marriage between baptized people is not only under the law of God but also under the law of the Church, without prejudice to the competence of the civil authority with regard to the purely civil consequences." This point of view is at least several centuries old. Where baptized Christians are concerned, the Church is competent in everything that has to do with the marital bond itself and whatever is necessarily associated with it, such as the legitimacy of the children. In cases of this nature, the State is only competent in such matters as property, inheritance, etc.

There is a problem here which also occurs in other fields as in the question of interest and the question of religious freedom. Is the refusal to recognize the validity of State law an absolutely valid dogmatic truth, or is it simply a point of view which is conditioned by certain past historical circumstances and, therefore, just as changeable as the historical circumstances themselves? Papal statements about the exclusive validity of the Church's marriage ordinances are relatively recent. The first usually quoted was promulgated by Pius VI on August 28, 1794. These statements were aimed at opinions that would have denied the competence of the Church altogether or that wanted to separate the marriage contract from the sacrament, as well as at other similar misconceptions. Over against these the popes confirmed the validity of Church law as it was understood at that time. The main speculative argument for the exclusive competence of the Church remains the sacramental character of a valid marriage between two baptized Christians and the sacred character of a marriage between a baptized person and a nonbaptized one.

St. Thomas looked at this problem differently. He distinguished between the several purposes of marriage, each of which has its own, different legal aspect. As a means to procreation, marriage is subject to the law implied in human nature itself; as ordered toward the welfare of the political community, it is subject to civil law; as ordered toward the welfare of the Church, it is subservient to Church law (*Summa contra Gentiles,* 4, 78). This view seems to come much closer to the heart of the matter. Marriage, even marriage between Christians, is not only sacramental or sacred. It is also an earthly, secular reality. The Church's mission, and therefore its competence, is in itself an exclusively religious one. But it is easy to see why in earlier centuries people entrusted the ecclesiastical authorities with ordering much that was not religious, and the Church accepted this situation. This is certainly part of its human, historical mission, but not of its Christian mission which is valid for all ages.

Today we have a better understanding of the autonomy of secular values and hence of the State's political and juridical autonomy with regard to Church order. In marriage, then, should not the Church confine itself to the religious aspects and leave the ordering of the earthly, temporal and secular aspects to the political community? This has already happened on one point, at least in practice. In the case of a baptized person the Church recognizes as valid the various legal regulations concerning the impediment of legal affinity which arises from adoption. Is not a similar arrangement indicated regarding all other impediments which have no religious implications, such as blood-relationship, affinity, public respectability, age and abduction? Impediments of this nature were inspired by social conditions; they did not arise from religious motives. Is it even necessary to legalize the various civil laws on these points for Catholics by Church law? Can we not simply recognize that in the matter of marriage a Catholic is also subject to legitimate civil authority?

A Catholic who wants to share in the sacramental and liturgical life as a member of the Church will obviously remain subject to its laws. The Church must uphold the scriptural and

natural norms pertaining to marriage. In this regard it is exclusively competent. This includes, for instance, the ecclesiastical
celebration, impediments arising from ordination, vows, mixed
marriage and—if we wish to maintain this—spiritual affinity.
The State does not have to sanction this Church order; it must
only recognize and guarantee the freedom to apply it and not
impose upon Catholics, or others, any regulations that go against
their conscience.

This leads to another question. Today the Church law, including its regulations concerning marriage, applies in principle also
to non-Catholic baptized Christians. The only exception has to
do with the ecclesiastical form of the celebration and the invali-
dating impediment of "disparity of cult". All other positive ecclesiastical regulations concerning the way in which consent
must be declared, the impediments, the renewal of the consent
required for the convalidation of an invalid contract and similar
regulations take for granted that they are also binding on non-
Catholic baptized Christians. This leads to curious consequences.
Thus, a Protestant can contract a valid marriage with a non-
Christian but not with his Christian grand-niece! Moreover,
theoretical and practical considerations play a part in this, considerations which are now definitely out of date after the Council. Early theologians saw in the baptismal character a kind of
indelible stamp impressed on the soul, thereby making it the
inalienable property of Christ and subjecting it once and for all
to the authority of the Church. (This view is now also called the
"juridical" view, referring to the incorrect sense in which it is
now often used in ecclesiastical circles.) A non-Catholic baptized
Christian was considered as someone who was obliged to become Catholic and to submit himself to the Church's laws.
Then, if a non-Catholic Christian was not validly married, there
always remained the possibility of his being received into the
Catholic Church and contracting marriage with a member of
the Catholic faith. It is a pity that this totally untenable attitude
is still to be found in recent publications.

A radical revision is absolutely necessary. Certainly the

Church can judge the marriages of non-Catholic baptized Christians by standards based on natural law and scripture. But the legislation of *positive* ecclesiastical ordinances for people who are in no position to recognize or even know these laws is clearly an antiquated practice.

In this connection one may even wonder whether the refusal of a church celebration must always have as a result for the Catholic party that he can no longer validly marry the other party. It is understandable that an ecclesiastical celebration is considered unsuitable when a Catholic who wants to contract a mixed marriage at the same time rejects any obligation to educate his children in the Catholic way. But does this mean that he must be barred from contracting a non-ecclesiastical valid marriage? The recent instruction of the Congregation for the Doctrine on the Faith about mixed marriages seems to leave room for this possibility.

5. *Marital Disposition and Positive Church Law*

The urgency of this question is revealed when we look at it from another angle. A person can always claim that his marriage is not valid, even after years of living together with genuine marital intent, and even if in the meanwhile he has assumed the responsibilities of parenthood. A Catholic who has only contracted a civil marriage is always free, according to canon law, to leave his spouse and children and to contract another, ecclesiastical marriage. All he needs is a declaration from his bishop stating that he is "free". Catholic marriages not infrequently also break up even after years of marital life, usually because of an extra-marital relationship. Only then does one begin to look for a cause to prove the existing marriage invalid. Sometimes the search is successful, and it is usually found that the marriage was contracted either under duress or without full consent. Occasionally the purely formal objection is raised that the priest who assisted at the marriage was not validly delegated. If proved this can become grounds for annulment, thereby freeing the parties to contract valid Christian marriages.

It is generally agreed that this situation is untenable. Church law must not declare that people are validly married between whom there is no full Christian marital disposition. On the other hand, where this disposition *does* exist, the Church should not offer married couples the opportunity to abandon each other and their family on grounds that are unacceptable from the Christian point of view but are accidentally covered by positive legal regulations that really have nothing to do with the real situation. Moreover, Church law should not—as is now often the practice—identify nullity in positive law with freedom to contract a new marriage. The law can just as well contain an obligation to repeal the nullity and turn the relationship into a valid marriage.

Now we come to some suggestions that may lead to a decline in cases of nullity in positive law concerning the impediments, the canonical form and the convalidation of an non-valid marriage.

(a) *The Impediments.* Cases of nullification based on a nullifying impediment seem to be extremely rare. Hence, in the present discussion they can be passed over. Nonetheless, I would like to make one important observation. Nowadays one would like to see the so-called impediments of lesser degree (canon 1042) abolished. This would include marital infidelity (*crimen*), namely, adultery incurred upon contracting an invalid marriage. In practice it comes down to this: a civil marriage contracted after divorce cannot be convalidated after the death of the lawful partner without a dispensation. Is it really desirable that this impediment be abolished without any further ado? It does not seem quite so obvious that both the ecclesiastical community and the "notorious" adulterers should simply have to await the death of the lawful partner in order to turn an adulterous relationship into a Christian marriage. It would appear that a more serious pastoral approach is required here, not merely in the public interest insofar as witness to the Christian community is concerned, but also, and more so, for the sake of the religious attitude of those concerned.

(b) *The Canonical Form.* Suggestions on this point differ widely. On the one hand, there are those who wish to maintain the canonical form, and this as a requisite for validity, but they wish to modify the form in such a way that there is less risk of the priest who assists at the marriage not being authorized to do so. Before introducing such modifications one ought to first find out whether they are necessary. As far as I know, processes of nullification based on unauthorized assistance hardly ever occur, if at all. The main problem here concerns marriages, principally mixed marriages contracted outside the Church.

On the other hand, some have suggested that the form which is valid according to civil legislation should also be recognized as applying to Catholics, possibly as an alternative to the canonical form and followed by an ecclesiastical blessing. The Council of Trent introduced the canonical form as the only alternative to a clandestine marriage. This no longer exists. The alternative is now either an ecclesiastical marriage or a civil one. In principle there is no objection why civil marriages cannot be recognized as valid even for Catholics. However, there are serious consequences. Once the canonical form disappeared there would be no further guarantee of pastoral preparation for marriage. This might produce more frequent uncertainty about full consent; impediments might in large part lose their social validity, particularly those that are merely forbidden; it would be very difficult to have a reliable ecclesiastical registration, and therefore it would become similarly difficult to establish the "free status" of the partners. Finally, in actual fact the canonical form is also the liturgical form. Is the Church not the most appropriate place in which to celebrate a marriage in Christ? These objections are partly countered by the suggestion that both forms should be recognized as valid but that the canonical form should be made obligatory, possibly under pain of excommunication. But even this is not really very satisfactory. Would it not be best to maintain the canonical form, but to leave the recognition of the civilly valid forms open in those cases where from the pastoral point of view this is recommended procedure?

(c) *Convalidation of Invalid Marriages.* There is not much enthusiasm for suggestions that would introduce legalization of invalid relationships, for example, after a certain period of co-habitation or after the birth of a child. This would mean that many relationships where there is not, nor ever will be, any gen-uine disposition for marriage would be transformed into canon-ically valid marriages. Such blanket measures which exclude personal pastoral care are definitely not desirable, unless in the case of purely formal and juridical impediments such as *bona fide* unauthorized assistance or such nullifying impediments which have nothing to do with the marital disposition.

The Motu Proprio *Pastorale munus* of November 30, 1963, nn. 21-22, gives the local ordinaries the authority to legalize marriages that have been contracted only before the civil author-ity. This has not yet been put into practice sufficiently in certain regions. Moreover, a new Church order could reduce consider-ably the demands for a "simple convalidation". Would it not be a good thing to authorize local ordinaries to use broader powers, such as the power of dispensation in the case of ecclesiastical impediments and, particularly, the power to adjust the canonical form to various circumstances, for instance, in some cases simply requiring the assistance of a priest? On the other hand, one should not engage in *sanatio* (legalization) or convalidation when one is not sure of a true marital disposition.

6. *The Legal Processes*

Various measures have been suggested to ensure that mar-riage processes are dealt with more efficiently, to make sure that cases are judged by competent authorities, to reduce the expenses of legal aid and to prevent abuses, particularly in the case of a canonical nullification that is either irrelevant to the real situation or even a mere fiction. Such measures are obviously most op-portune, but I am personally convinced that a really satisfactory Church law will demand much more radical revision. As long as we cling to the present legal procedure in these cases with its courts, its dossiers (and their translation!), its judicial instances (at least two, and a third one for the Rota), and so on, the situation of people who think they have a claim to deliverance from a marriage that is already shattered will remain extremely painful. Is it not already an anomalous situation that in the Church strictly legal disputes, like all other business, are dealt with administratively by episcopal curias and Roman congregations, while in practice only the delicate and very personal issues about the validity of marriage are brought before courts of justice? We might add that in this way the question about the validity or nullity of a marriage (which is always abstract) becomes completely detached from its pastoral context, from decisions that must be made in a Christian way depending upon the concrete situation and from the mutual responsibility of the two partners toward each other and toward their children. Pastoral collaboration in the search for a responsible solution in case of doubt is excluded—and how often are the judges themselves not in doubt? Judges can only choose between the *constat* or *non constat* (the existence or non-existence) of nullity. They cannot get away from that inexorable canon 1014!

It is understandable that in days gone by, when the Church had to take charge of a large part of the social order and when its judgment about a marriage had consequences which affected property, inheritance and other secular or social aspects, there was a need for rigorous legal procedure. Nowadays almost everywhere the Church's judgment only concerns the religious and ecclesiastical situation, and this requires a radically different approach.

First of all, it cannot really be impossible to train sufficient priests—and why not also laymen?—in at least the larger dioceses or ecclesiastical provinces in such a way that they are capable of investigating and judging in a satisfactory and reliable manner whether a marriage is canonically valid or not, without requiring the intervention of further authorities. Of course, such an investigation would be bound by norms that are essential to reach a reliable conclusion, but it would not need any further forensic formalities. Furthermore, such a canonical judgment would not be detached from a genuine pastoral care for those concerned; rather, it would be an integral part of it. Those concerned should naturally have the opportunity to appeal to a higher authority, and it would remain necessary to draft and preserve a written justification for the decisions reached. It is possible to provide regular supervision—by Rome, if necessary —through an annual report, visitation or the like in order to correct too much severity or too much broadmindedness. For the moment there is no point in going into detail. The main question concerns two points: canonical investigation both as an investigation on the spot, at least normally, and as part of general pastoral care.

My personal conviction that revision of marriage law will have to proceed along these or similar lines does not imply that I am unaware of possible powerful opposition, but I am sufficiently convinced to expect other things as well.

BIOGRAPHICAL NOTES

JOSEPH LECLER, S.J.: Born during October, 1895, in Cherbourg, France, he became a Jesuit and was ordained in 1927. He pursued his studies at the Ecole des Hautes Etudes and the Scholasticat de Fourvier in Lyons, and earned his doctorate in theology in 1931. He has been editor of the review *Etudes* since 1930, and was professor of the theological faculty of the Institut Catholique in Paris from 1938 to 1960. Since 1950 he has been director of *Recherches de Science religieuse*. His published works in French include books on Church and State, tolerance and the Reformation which was translated into English in 1960, and the history of the Ecumenical Council of Vienna (1311-1312).

RABBI ARTHUR GILBERT: Born June 4, 1926, in Philadelphia, he earned a degree in letters in 1947 at New York University, and in Hebrew and rabbinical studies at the Jewish Institute of Religion. From 1951 to 1954 he pursued further studies in psychology and psychoanalysis. In his post as director of the National Department of Interreligious Cooperation, he worked for better relations between the Jewish community and Protestants, Catholics and Moslems. Since 1965 he has been director of the National Department of Interreligious Curriculum Research and of the Anti-Defamation League of B'nai B'rith. Among his published works are *The Jews in Christian America* (1966), *Currents and Trends in Contemporary Jewish Thought* (1966), *Religion and the Public Order* (1964), and many contributions to reviews such as *Editorial Board, Reconstructionist* and the *Journal of Ecumenical Studies*. Scheduled for publication in the near future is a study entitled *The Vatican Council and the Jews*.

PIETRO PAVAN: Born in 1903 in Povegliano, Italy, he was ordained in 1928 for the diocese of Treviso. He studied at the Gregorian University in Rome and at the University of Padua, earning degrees in philosophy in 1930, in theology in 1932, and in economic and social sciences in 1935 at Padua. He presently teaches social economics at Lateran University. Among his published works in Italian are books on the social order, democracy, the laity today and religious liberty.

LUKAS VISCHER: Born November 23, 1926, in Switzerland, he earned his doctorate in theology in 1952 at the University of Basel. From 1953 to 1961 he was pastor of the Reformed Church at Schaffhausen, Switzerland. Since 1961 he has been Research Secretary for the Faith and Order Department of the World Council of Churches. He was an official observer for the World Council at Vatican Council II. His published works include *Basilius the Great* (1952) and *The History of Confirmation*

181

(1958). At present he is editor of a series of studies being published by the Evangelical Church Press in Zurich.

✠ NEOPHYTOS EDELBY: Born November, 1920 in Alep, Syria, he pursued his studies at the Lateran University and at the Institutum Utriusque Iuris, both in Rome. He earned his doctorate "in utroque iure" in 1950. He was a professor in the Seminary of St. Anne in Jerusalem, then Secretary of the Holy Synod of the Greek-Melkite Church, and finally was consecrated titular archbishop of Edessa and appointed advisor to Patriarch Maximos IV. His published works include a book on the Byzantine missal and contributions to encyclopedias and reviews, especially *Proche-Orient Chrétien*.

JACQUES VROEMEN: Born in 1936 in Heerlen, the Netherlands, he studied at the Catholic University at Nijmegen and earned a degree in cultural anthropology in 1962. Further studies followed at the International Institute of Social Studies at La Haye. He participated in the work of the Center of African Studies at Leyde, the Netherlands, in 1965, and is presently at the Institute of Cultural Anthropology at Nijmegen. He is a regular contributor to Dutch reviews.

JOSEPH MASSON, S.J.: Born September 21, 1908, in Montigny, France, he became a Jesuit and was ordained in 1938. After philosophical and theological studies at Louvain, he attended the Institut Orientaliste of the University of Louvain. He earned a doctorate in philosophy, a licentiate in theology and a doctorate in Oriental philosophy and history. Because of his knowledge of the last-named field, he has been called upon to occupy various posts such as Director of the Indian Section at Notre Dame de la Paix in Namur, professor on the Faculty of Missiology of Gregorian University, professor at the Jesuit College at Louvain in addition to several posts at the University of Louvain, and consultor to the Secretariat for Non-Christians. Among his published works are many contributions to collective works, as well as articles on theology and missionary methodology. At present he is writing a commentary on the *Decree on the Church's Missionary Activity* of Vatican Council II.

TEODORO JIMÉNEZ-URRESTI: Born April 1, 1924, in Bilbao, Spain, he was ordained for that diocese in 1949. Studies at the Gregorian and the Lateran Universities in Rome led to a licentiate in dogmatic theology and a doctorate in canon law and Roman law. At present he is professor of dogmatic theology and Diocesan General Pro-Vicar. His published works include books in Spanish and numerous contributions to scholarly journals.

PETRUS HUIZING, S.J.: Born February 22, 1911, he became a Jesuit and was ordained in 1942. After studying at the University of Louvain, the Gregorian University in Rome and the University of Munich, he earned his doctorate in civil law in 1938 and in canon law in 1947. From 1946 to 1952 he was professor of canon law at the University of Maastricht, and from 1952 to 1964 at the Gregorian University in Rome.

IVAN ŽUŽEK, S.J.: Born September 2, 1924, in Ljubljana, Yugoslavia, he became a Jesuit and was ordained in 1955. He pursued his studies at the Pontifical Oriental Institute, and he earned a licentiate in canon law at the Gregorian University in Rome. He has been professor of Oriental canon law at the Oriental Institute since 1963. His published works include *Studies on the Chief Code of Russian Canon Law* and contributions to *Orientalia Christiana Periodica*.

International Publishers of CONCILIUM

ENGLISH EDITION
Paulist Press
Glen Rock, N. J., U.S.A.

Burns & Oates Ltd
25 Ashley Place
London, S.W.1

DUTCH EDITION
Uitgeverij Paul Brand, N. V.
Hilversum, Netherlands

FRENCH EDITION
Maison Mame
Tours/Paris, France

GERMAN EDITION
Verlagsanstalt Benziger & Co., A.G.
Einsiedeln, Switzerland

Matthias Grunewald-Verlag
Mainz, W. Germany

SPANISH EDITION
Ediciones Guadarrama
Madrid, Spain

PORTUGUESE EDITION
Livraria Morais Editora, Ltda.
Lisbon, Portugal

ITALIAN EDITION
Editrice Queriniana
Brescia, Italy